Winning Trust and Confidence

A Grounded Theory Model

A. Bazin

DEDICATION

In starting this project, I never could have imagined just how challenging a journey it would eventually become. I could have not accomplished a project of this magnitude alone. Simply, I would have failed years ago if it were not for the support of my loved ones. I would like to thank my wife, Julie, and my children, Ryan and Emily. You have been there for me through it all, and I dedicate this project to you because without you it would not have happened. You are my life and my inspiration. Thank you.

ACKNOWLEDGEMENTS

I would like to thank the dissertation committee Doctors, Peggy Sundstrom, Amy Hakim, and Kristin Ballard. Your support in this effort has been phenomenal, and by taking the time to guide me along the way, you have changed my life for the better. I will never forget the sacrifice and your personal commitment to excellence and high standards. You have shaped my identity as a scholar for life and, more importantly, shaped me as a person for the better, thank you. Dr. Sundstrom, simply, there is no way I could have done this without your wise advice, thank you so much.

I would like to thank the institutions that contributed to this effort. Fort Leavenworth's Combat Studies Institute and their Operational Leadership Experiences database laid the foundation for my project. Additionally, the University of the Rockies has gained my undying gratitude for support and for developing an institution where ideas and people can grow. It is unique in its high standards, which I will aspire to live up to for the rest of my life.

Finally, for those who volunteered for this project, thank you. My desire is that your efforts, experience, and hard work will inform future generations of soldiers ultimately making themselves and the nation successful.

TABLE OF CONTENTS

Abstract iii

Dedication iv

Acknowledgements...v

Table of Contents vi

List of Tables viii

List of Figures ix

List of Appendices..x

CHAPTER I: INTRODUCTION 1

General Statement...1

Statement of the Problem..4

Purpose of the Study 6

Importance of the Study 7

Conceptual Framework 9

Research Questions 11

Overview of Research Design 12

Definition of Key Terms..14

Assumptions, Limitations, and Delimitations...15

Summary 17

CHAPTER II: LITERATURE REVIEW 19

Search Strategy 19

Conceptual Origins 20

Perspectives from the Political Science and International Relations Field.......................20

Perspectives from the Psychology Field 26

Perspectives from the Conflict Resolution Field 31

Narrowing the Context: The U.S. Military's Operational Environment 32

Relevant Military Publications 35

CHAPTER III: METHOD...38

Methodology Selected 39

Study Participants 41

Data Collection 45

Procedures Followed 46

Trustworthiness and Transferability 49

Ethical Concerns 53

Data Analysis 55

CHAPTER IV: RESULTS 60

Sample 60

Data Collection 63

Data Analysis and Results 65

CHAPTER V: DISCUSSION 87

Interpretation of Findings 88

Limitations of Study 93

Implications for Theory and Research...96

Recommendations for Further Research..101

Conclusion 103

References 105

LIST OF TABLES

Table 1. Trust Models 31

Table 2. Initial Sample Demographics 61

Table 3. Subject Mater Expert Sample Demographics 63

Table 4. Open Coding Initial Results 66

Table 5. Codes Classified by Major Theme 72

Table 6. Major Themes Ordered by Frequency 73

Table 7. Major Theme Connections 74

Table 8. Major Theme Triangulation with Literature Review 75

Table 9. Deliberate Confidence-building Measures Used 79

Table 10. Suggestions for Future Service Members 81

Table 11. Theoretical Model Comments 82

Table 12. Open-ended Question 83

LIST OF FIGURES

Figure 1. Summary of Bio-psychological Research on Trust...29

Figure 2. Research Design 38

Figure 3. Venn Diagram Depicting the Sample..45

Figure 4. Initial Theoretical Model..75

Figure 5. Model for Expert Triangulation..76

Figure 6. Confidence-building Measure Use in the Contemporary Environment...........85

Figure 7. Examples of Confidence-building Measures..85

Figure 8. Confidence-building Measures Lessons Learned...86

LIST OF APPENDICES

A. Signed Permission Letter 117

B. Informed Consent Form 118

C. Subject Matter Expert Interview Framework..120

D. Subject Matter Expert Contact Email 121

CHAPTER I: INTRODUCTION

In the contemporary world, the United States asks its service members to do much more than simply fight its wars. In a counterinsurgency-type environment, such as in Iraq and Afghanistan, indigenous partners that the service member is training or supporting one day may be the very ones that use violence to oppose them the next. Numerous authors in the conflict resolution field have discussed resolving protracted conflicts through the application of small confidence-building measures over time to reassure the other party of one's peaceful intentions (Furlong, 2005; Landau & Landau, 1997; Sandole, Byrne, Sandole-Staroste, & Senehi, 2009). The researcher employed a qualitative methodology to learn from those who have experienced the phenomena of confidence-building in Iraq or Afghanistan and, subsequently, constructed a theoretical model of confidence-building measure employment for future use by service members.

The introductory chapter will cover the overall nature of the dissertation. This includes a general statement, statement of the problem, purpose of the study, importance of the study, theoretical framework, and research questions. This section will then discuss an overview of the research design; definition of terms; and assumptions, limitations, and delimitations. Finally, it will cover a brief summary of the introduction.

General Statement

Conflict is one characteristic of the human condition and exists at all levels of individual and group interaction. There are many theories that seek to explain why this is the case. Authors from the field of psychology have asserted that conflict in our lives is attributed to such things as frustration that leads to aggression (Fox & Spector, 1999), differences in gender (Rennison & Planty, 2003), presence of weapons or instruments of

1

violence (Wagstaff, MacVeigh, Boston, & Scott, et al., 2003), social learning (Wareham, Boots, & Chavez, 2009), mental illness, drug and alcohol use (Van Dorn, Williams, Del-Colle, & Hawkins, 2009), lack of communication (Giles, 2007), cognitive dissonance (Zepeda, 2006), ego (Rangell, 1969), and the biology and chemistry of the body (Webb, 1992).

In the realm of political science, authors have asserted that power inequalities (Braumoeller, 2008), power shifts, uncertainty, appeasement (Powell, 1996), class conflict (Olson, 2010), limited resources (Obi, 2010), rational choices (Fearon, 1995), or culture (Bhandar, 2008), all could play a factor in conflict. In the field of religious study, scholars view conflict distilled down to its simplest proximate cause, the interaction of good versus evil in the hearts of humans (Nolan & Burleigh, 2012). Mediation literature has focused on conflict originating from people's tendency to undertake positional bargaining (Moore, 2003). Conflict exists as a component of the human condition for many different reasons, and, when conflict reaches extremes, it can become harmful to all those involved.

Arguably, war is conflict in its worst and most destructive form. In war, the scale, scope, and destructive power of humans is extended to its most extreme and harmful level. As a collective, groups maximize their power over the lives of other human beings to force their will upon others. As a form of conflict, it is difficult for one to assert that war is in and of itself right or wrong. Without doubt, war creates anguish and suffering. However, it can also serve to prevent the emergence of the extremes in human ideology and negative group behavior. One can argue that examples of war have the unique ability to positively address societal problems, such as the rise of Germany's National Socialism during World War II,

Bosnian genocide in the 1990s, or forms violent Islamic extremism that exist in the world today (Gilpin, 1981).

The primary reason that the U.S. military exists is to fight and win the nation's wars. This primary purpose puts service members continually in harm's way to further the political and strategic goals of the nation. When these policy goals include supporting other partner nations in providing their own security, often more than just fighting required. People that are indigenous to the nation involved in the conflict become the critical variable. Instead of only fighting, service members are required to train military and police forces, work with local governments to increase their legitimacy and efficacy, and assist in the development of basic services. Hence, people become the mission, and it becomes increasingly necessary to build trust with these key indigenous stakeholders (Hunt, 1995).

From the terrorist attacks on the World Trade Center and the Pentagon through 2012, the United States military deployed 1,425,200 service members to Iraq or Afghanistan, with many service members having deployed multiple times (Belasco, 2009). Authors of numerous strategic forecasting works described the future operational environment for the military as one that will likely continue to require numerous troop deployments (Department of Defense, 2010; Friedman, 2009; National Intelligence Council, 2002). The U.S. may employ future service members on wide array of missions, many of which could necessitate building relationships with other military and civilian partners (Department of Defense, 2009).

Insights from the international relations, psychology, and conflict resolution fields of study indicated that parties in conflict can employ various measures over time to promote the belief that, in the future, each will act in a mutually beneficial manner (Osgood, 1959; Raju,

2009; Stimson Center, 2011; Vick, 1988). Often referred to as confidence-building measures, these measures are activities that can bring deep-rooted conflicts closer to positive resolution (Borawski, 1986; Burt, 1984; Higgins, 2001; Hilali, 2005; Maiese, 2003; Nation, 1989; Raju, 2009; Rathmell, 2000; Stimson Center, 2011; United Nations 1975; United Nations, 1986; UN Center for Disarmament, 1982). The researcher investigated the application confidence-building measures to address the operational need of present and future soldiers to succeed in the difficult mission of building trust.

Statement of the Problem

As a response to attacks of September 11, 2001, the U.S. has sent its military on long-term military operations in Iraq and Afghanistan. As these operations evolved, they took on the nature of counterinsurgencies. In such conflicts, positively influencing the will of the people becomes the military objective for parties on both sides of the conflict. The insurgent force requires a compliant population for survival. Simultaneously, the counterinsurgent must strive to gain public support to help legitimize governmental institutions. The struggle for popular support can become the center of gravity for the military operation, and it often takes years, even decades, to determine the victor (U.S. Army, 2006).

Nowhere is the complex nature of this problem more apparent than the recent insider attacks that have occurred in Afghanistan, where the host nation forces that the U.S. military trains attack them. The reason for these attacks is often difficult to ascertain and varies from incident to incident. However, the commonalities include: (a) a member of the local population volunteering to support the U.S., (b) the member of the population gaining access to a weapon, and (c) the member of the population turning on his U.S. counterparts. The Department of Defense has attributed only 15% of these attacks to a deliberate insurgent plan

4

(Morgenstein & Popalzai, 2013). From 2007 to 2012, there were 71 such attacks documented in Afghanistan, increasing from two in 2008, to 42 in 2012 (Hossain, 2012). Because the nature of the majority of these attacks is not directly attributable to any enemy plan, there exists the possibility of other causes. The U.S. has placed its service members in a precarious position where they must build trust and the potential ramifications of failure in the mission are dire. There is a degree of vulnerability in any relationship, but in a non-permissive and hostile environment, a lack of trust can lead to death of oneself or one's fellow service members.

As described by the Department of Defense (2012), there are numerous combat and non-combat missions envisioned for future armed forces. Many of these missions would require service members to deal with indigenous populations, often in a semi-permissive or non-permissive context. The future missions relevant to this research could include: (a) countering terrorism and irregular warfare, (b) deterring and defeating aggression, (c) providing a stabilizing presence, (d) conducting stability and counterinsurgency operations, and (e) conducting humanitarian, disaster relief, and other operations. Therefore, the possibility exists that military service members can expect to face this problem of trust building in the future.

More specifically, U.S. service members face a complex problem when building trust with key indigenous stakeholders in the contemporary operating environment, and the creation a theory, grounded in the data, that explains this phenomenon, might provide a useful framework that they can apply to accomplishing this difficult task. The focus of this study is an important problem worthy of study because too often following conflict, military forces reduce their size dramatically and forget the lessons of the past. Future generations of service members must then relearn past lessons. The impact of the research problem is that if this study can capture lessons learned and codify them in a theoretical model that service members can apply in future contexts, then service members can potentially avoid costly, potentially deadly, mistakes when building trust. This research study represented a unique approach to the research problem because no scholars have attempted a study of this subject and type with this population in this context.

This study addressed this specific research problem by contributing original findings to the academic knowledge of the conflict resolution field through the creation of a new theoretical model using grounded theory qualitative research. This study addressed this specific research problem by utilizing a grounded theory research methodology to discover a theoretical model of how U.S. soldiers built confidence with local civilian populations and host-nation military forces in Iraq and Afghanistan. Future deploying service members can use this theoretical model to guide their interactions with multiple stakeholders when building confidence is an operational imperative.

Purpose of the Study

The purpose of this grounded theory qualitative study was to build a new theory, grounded in data, to explain the phenomenon of military service members building trust with indigenous populations in Afghanistan and Iraq. This purpose addressed the research problem by directly investigating the phenomena of confidence-building and constructing a theoretical model. The central idea behind this study was that intuitively, and through trial-and-error, service members have used confidence-building measures to incrementally improve trust levels over time.

The initial units of analysis were perceived levels of trust, the measures they applied to build confidence, and time. However, since this study sought to formulate a theoretical model to describe phenomena, this study did not rule out any variable or unit of analysis prematurely. The approach to knowledge creation that this study sought was inductive, to develop general propositions derived from specific examples. The general methodology, qualitative, is also the best for this research because the existing body of knowledge given the context of the population, subject, and context of the problem is limited. If scholars knew more about the phenomena in this specific context a quantitative methodology would have been prudent. Given the nature of the research problem, this is not the case. For this type of qualitative study, it is important that this research clearly identify the phenomenon, situation, and factors of interest. The phenomenon upon which the researcher focused was the recent application of confidence-building measures by service members in Iraq and Afghanistan.

In Iraq and Afghanistan, the nature of the situation necessitated that service members focused on winning over the people, training local military and police forces, and enabling the indigenous population to provide for their own security. Without the trust of the people, the service member would simply not succeed in this task. The initial factors of interest were (a) the confidence-building measures that soldiers employed, (b) the overall level of trust they felt they achieved, and (c) the time it took to achieve this level of trust. However, the researcher did not seek to exclude any factors outright. The grounded theory methodology did not initially limit the scope of the research just to these initial factors.

Importance of the Study

The importance of this research is that service members have intuitively developed ways to build confidence through experience and trial and error with the local stakeholders they interact with when deployed to contingency operations. However, there is neither a unifying theoretical model nor academic work that has captured these experiences, generalized them, and made them useable for future generations of soldiers who will face similar circumstances. The unfortunate situation is that although there are many institutional mechanisms to collect lessons learned, there was no unifying body of knowledge on the subject of confidence-building. The military could lose these hard-earned lessons, and worse, the military may have to relearn the lessons on the future battlefield, a dangerous and costly prospect.

This study contributed to both theory and practice through improving the military's future effectiveness in three major ways. First, through the conduct of a rigorous qualitative analysis, this study separated the concept of confidence-building into its component parts so its conceptual and operational structure was clear. Second, this study described the interactions and relationships between these factors through development of a new theory, grounded in the data, which explains the phenomenon of interest. Finally, this study synthesized the existing body of knowledge about confidence-building measures to build a structure for wider understanding and application in the field. Simply, the purpose of this research was to take the idea of confidence-building measures, and, through applying academic rigor and research, construct a theoretical model, grounded in the data, that future service members could apply to accomplish a challenging mission more effectively.

The potential implications of this research are both academic and practical. First, there was no theoretical model for employing confidence-building measures that has taken the perspectives of the various academic fields of international relations, political science, psychology, and conflict resolution and unified them in a comprehensive way. Second, this study potentially increased usability of confidence-building measures for service members deployed to counterinsurgency, humanitarian relief, or other contingency operations where the interaction with host nation civilian and military leadership is essential to success.

This research sought a theoretical model grounded in data that captured current service member experiences. Deployed service members could use this theoretical model to build confidence more effectively and more efficiently, directly leading to application of the findings by a wider audience. Potentially, practitioners in the conflict resolution field could also benefit from a well-researched theoretical model that makes the idea of confidence-building easy to understand and employ.

Conceptual Framework

This study concerned confidence-building measures, which the fields of international relations, political science, conflict resolution, and psychology, all conceptually address. Literature from studies in these fields has indicated that the effectiveness of confidence-building measures was a function of time and the methods employed and additionally suggested that one could validate the existence of this relationship through research involving subjects experienced with building trust.

First, through the identification of each author's recommended techniques for confidence-building and the major categories of these techniques, one can observe generalized typology. The literature review indicated that one can divide the types of confidence-building measures into major subcategories. The first subcategory is communication measures, such as exchanges of information that the parties in conflict perceive as positive (Hilali, 2005; Maiese, 2003; Nation, 1989; Osgood, 1959; Raju, 2009; Stimson Center, 2011; Vick, 1988). The second category of confidence-building measures is physical measures, such as tangible activities or limits on activities that the parties in conflict understand and are predictable (Borawski, 1986; Burt, 1984; Higgins, 2001; Hilali, 2005; Maiese, 2003; Nation, 1989; Raju, 2009; Rathmell, 2000; Stimson Center, 2011, 1986; United Nations, 1975; United Nations, 1982; UN Center for Disarmament, 1982; United Nations, 1986; Vick, 1988). The third major category is economic measures that lead to the belief that the allocation of resources is mutually beneficial (Higgins, 2001; Kahn, 2010; Raju, 2009; UN Center for Disarmament, 1982). The fourth major category is political measures that include formulation, recognition, and adherence to agreements (Gottwald, Hasenclever & Kamis, 2009; Hilali, 2005; Kahn, 2010; Maiese, 2003; Muniruzzaman, 2010; Raju, 2009; UN Center for Disarmament, 1982; UN Office for Disarmament, 2009; Vick, 1988). The fifth major category is relationship measures that include interpersonal interactions that leave a positive impression (Kahn, 2010; Maiese, 2003; Ota, 2009; UN Center for Disarmament, 1982; UN Office for Disarmament, 2009; United Nations, 1982). The sixth major category of confidence-building measures identified is planning activities that lead to the development of a shared vision for the future (Gottwald et al., 2009; Higgins, 2001).

Literature from the psychology field provided insight into how parties build trust at the one-on-one level and provided insight into another critical variable, time. From the humanistic perspective, because safety is a common need for all (Maslow, 1954), safety is a starting point because, in conflict, one party's need for safety is interdependent with the other's. Rogers' (1980) core conditions describe how, at a personal level, parties can build a level of confidence and human connection. From a humanistic perspective, confidence-building works because it creates encounters (Rowan, 2001) between people where they

10

interact in a reciprocally positive manner and are a function of the number of encounters over time. From the cognitive-behavioral perspective (Wright, Basco, & Thase, 2006), people, including those in conflict, iteratively go through the stages of (a) event, (b) cognitive appraisal (including automatic thoughts), (c) emotion, and, finally, (d) behavior.

Confidence-building measures help restructure the cognitive appraisal and positively influence resulting behavior. From the bio-psychological view of trust building, recent research (Dimoka, 2010; Kruger et al., 2007) has indicated that the brain accesses a level of distrust, conditional trust, or trust over time and then reacts both chemically and neurologically. Once one makes a decision to trust, the brain releases the powerful chemical oxytocin (the same neuro-chemical compound released when a new mother breastfeeds a baby), which strengthens the bond and increasingly makes it difficult to reverse (Evans, Shergill, & Averbeck, 2011).

Specifically, the conceptual framework of this topic originated from numerous fields, and the researcher sought to apply the concept of confidence-building measures to a new population and a new context. This multi-disciplinary approach to the literature review provided a solid foundational basis upon which to proceed toward the creation of a more in-depth theoretical model.

Research Questions

This study sought to refine knowledge using an a posteriori approach through the analysis of accounts of service members in context. The guiding research question which reflected the purpose statement of this research was, "What is a theory, grounded in the data, that explains how U.S. service members apply confidence building measures to build trust with key indigenous stakeholders in the contemporary joint operational environment?" The researcher used the following sub-questions to gain insight and subsequently to construct a grounded theory model:

1. What do the data indicate are the key qualitative statements that provide insight into how U.S. service members use confidence-building measures to build trust with key indigenous stakeholders in the contemporary joint operational environment?

2. What do the data indicate as the major categorical themes of how U.S. service members use confidence-building measures to build trust with key indigenous stakeholders in the contemporary joint operational environment?

3. What do the data indicate is the relationship between these major themes of how U.S. service members apply confidence-building measures to build trust with key indigenous stakeholders in the contemporary joint operational environment?

Overview of Research Design

The researcher employed a qualitative grounded theory approach to develop a theoretical model of confidence-building measure employment. Purposive theoretical sampling characterizes the grounded theory approach to research (Glaser, 1998). The Operational Leadership Experiences Database contained 2,515 interviews with service members with experience in Iraq and Afghanistan. The researcher utilized this existing collection to identify interviews where the terms "confidence" and "trust" are used and included data collected after 2008. Search results were screened to ensure the subjects' experience dates fell within the five-year parameters of 2008 to 2012. Open coding was used to screen context of search results to ensure that the data fit within the context of building confidence and trust with indigenous stakeholders in Iraq and Afghanistan.

The researcher uploaded all transcript files to the NVivo qualitative data analysis platform and conducted theoretical coding of data using NVivo software with memoing throughout to connect concepts and key ideas that helped formulate the theory at the conclusion of the study. This step of the research put special emphasis on the causes, contexts, contingencies, consequences, co-variance, and conditions that emerged from the data. The focus of the data coding was to identify types of confidence-building measures applied, identify and code other variables, group types into classification areas, and identify any other related variables that emerged. Additionally during coding, the researcher identified subject matter experts to assist in model verification. Then the researcher sorted and developed a theoretical outline that connected the data in a comprehensive theoretical model.

Next, the researcher conducted a literature review triangulation. This included uploading the text of the literature review into the NVivo program. The NVivo software was used to code and triangulate the literature review findings with the theoretical model, and to conduct memoing. Next, the theoretical model was refined to ensure it captured all of the major types of confidence-building measures, and consolidated findings into a revised version of the model.

Once the theoretical model had been refined, it was validated by subject matter experts. The researcher contacted potential experts asking for their voluntary participation and completion of the informed consent form. Then the researcher conducted interviews with each volunteer and uploaded each file of each interview into the NVivo program. The observations of the subject matter experts were codes, and the theoretical model was adjusted based on the perceptions and statements of the respondents.

This particular research design was the most appropriate to address the goals of the study because the overarching objective of this research is to create a new theoretical model for use in one specific context. The grounded theory approach was well suited to theoretical model development because it did not presuppose conclusions; it allowed the theory to emerge from the data inductively, which allowed the research to capture all variables that affected the phenomenon. In addition, the nature of the phenomena that this research sought to describe was not easily quantifiable as it concerned human perceptions and beliefs. Therefore, the qualitative approach, and specifically the grounded theory method of research design, was the most prudent.

Overall, the qualitative approach seeks to describe the meaning that each individual's behavior has for him or her in context of lived experience (Angus, 2000). This type of research is best suited for use when one seeks to understand human emotions, such as in the case with this research and the qualities of trust. In addition, because the qualitative methodology allows theoretical implications to emerge from the data, it increases the validity of the findings to the real world. Overall, the qualitative approach was best suited to this research because the ultimate goal of this research was to create a usable theoretical model that uses inductive logic to describe human emotion and behavior.

Definition of Key Terms

The way that people define and verbalize concepts is central to how they perceive and make sense of a very complex world (Chomsky, 1982). Therefore, definition of conceptual and operational central ideas is important. First, trust can be defined as "a psychological state comprising the intention to accept vulnerability based upon positive expectations of the intentions or behavior of another" (Rousseau et al., 1998, p. 395). One can conceptually define confidence-building measures as activities that can bring conflicts closer to positive resolution through promotion of the belief that, in the future, each party will act in a mutually beneficial manner (Borawski, 1986; Burt, 1984; Higgins, 2001; Hilali, 2005; Osgood, 1959; Raju, 2009; Stimson Center, 2011; Vick, 1988; United Nations 1975).

Definition of the population referred to as service members is also critical. This research defined service members as members of the U.S. armed forces including Army, Navy, Air Force, Marines, or Coast guard (The Judge Advocate General's School, 2006). This wider definition was important because not all of those deployed to Afghanistan and Iraq were from the Army or Marines. Numerous Air Force, Navy, and even Coast Guard officers worked at key positions that may have had beneficial insights as well.

The researcher looked at confidence-building measures with respect to the context of the contemporary joint operational environment. The joint services definition of the joint operational environment is the "composite of the conditions, circumstances, and influences that affect the employment of capabilities and bear on the decisions of the commander" (Department of Defense, 2011, p. GL-14). These definitions were the baseline for this research.

Assumptions, Limitations, and Delimitations

This research necessarily made assumptions in numerous areas. First, the researcher assumed that the sample of military service members surveyed represented the aggregate experiences of other service members to validate the theoretical model. The second major assumption was that the respondents answered questions without hindsight bias and intent to deceive. With qualitative research, one risk is that respondents will be biased to give answers that they feel are socially desirable. Goffman (1959) asserted that in social situations, people play "roles" to manage the impressions others have of them, and that people define truth in social, not absolute terms. He asserted that people conceal facts within what they express and that researchers can obtain insights into the validity of interviews indirectly through involuntary expressive behavior. Raffel (2013) has asserted that, even though Goffman's theory has its critics, it remains a valid construct. Therefore, assuming that Goffman's thesis is accurate, the researcher used in-depth, follow-up questions to capture rich qualitative data with the overall purpose of forming understanding from not only what the subjects said, but also what they meant on a deeper level. Third, there was an assumption that those who participated had sufficient experience and exposure to confidence-building measures to respond thoughtfully. There is an additional assumption that conflict has universal attributes and wide applicability, and that parties in conflict share similar characteristics, thereby enabling valid cross application and wider generalization of the theoretical model that emerged from this research.

One of the significant limitations of this study was that collection of accurate data from all sides involved in conflict is extremely difficult, and in the case of recent conflicts such as Iraq and Afghanistan, extremely dangerous. Another limitation was that only U.S. service members made up the sample. The researcher addressed only the context of the military's Joint Operating Environment. In addition, the researcher utilized references from numerous authors and experiences from individual service member, each of which contained unknown and undiscoverable biases and assumptions. Because of these limitations, the researcher could not assume that the theoretical model is without flaw. This means that if service members are to employ the theoretical model successfully in the future, they must first analyze the context of their unique situation. Confidence-building mechanisms may not address larger underlying issues in future conflict scenarios, and, at best are only one part of a conflict resolution solution.

The researcher made a few important delimitations to make answering the research question achievable. First, the study looked only at service member experiences in Iraq or

Afghanistan. There are many places that the U.S. can deploy service members; however, Iraq and Afghanistan represented the two most significant locations in recent history. This provided specificity to the findings, narrowing them to include experiences where conflict was the most dangerous and arguably most important. The second major delimitation of the study was the sample characteristics. Ideally, this research would have included subjects on both sides of the conflict and have included perspectives before, during, and after stakeholders attempted to employ confidence-building measures.

Practically, the conduct of academic research in a combat environment in situ includes a high-level of inherent risk to the safety of the researcher and, potentially, the subjects. To reduce this risk, the researcher necessarily investigated service members who returned to the U.S. from these environments. Another limiting factor of this study was the timeframe of experiences. The United States has deployed soldiers since 2002 to Iraq and Afghanistan. This research sought to capture the most recent and relevant accounts. Therefore, the researcher collected only data where the service member experienced the phenomenon during the period of 2008 to 2012, the past five years. These limiting factors were integral to the design and conduct of this research, and allowed this research to capture the data in a systematic manner.

Summary

Conflict is a pervasive part of the human condition for many reasons. Conflict in its extreme form, war, has many negative aspects but also serves a purpose in contemporary society. The U.S. charges its military with the task of fighting and winning the nation's wars, and increasingly, this means working with militaries and civilians from partner nations. Therefore, building trust with these partners becomes critical to mission success. The overarching purpose of this study was to understand the experiences of military service members who have had rich experiences building trust over time with indigenous populations in Afghanistan and Iraq and to develop a theoretical model grounded in the data for future use. The research proceeded using a qualitative methodology to define this theoretical model and verify it through triangulation of the findings with both the literature and subject matter experts.

This introductory chapter has summarized the key components and general direction that the researcher took. Subsequent chapters will discuss these subjects in detail providing more fidelity and context to the research. The literature that comprises the accepted body of academic knowledge on the topic of confidence-building is diverse and many different opinions, insights, and research form the foundation for this study. The literature review in the next section discusses exactly what this foundation is as a point of departure for creation of original academic knowledge.

CHAPTER II: LITERATURE REVIEW

The purpose of this literature review is to provide a comprehensive and exhaustive review of the relevant academic sources. This literature review covers the most important existing theories and research findings relevant to the research topic. The majority of primary sources on the topic fell within the realm of the political science and international relations fields; therefore, the majority of the references used reflect this fact. The study presents a literature review organized into four major sections that trace the concept of confidence-building measures through time in the political science and international relations field of study. The literature review then looks at the views of the psychology field and finally the literature that details the context of military trust building.

Search Strategy

The academic and non-academic search engines that this literature review used included: (a) Google, (b) Google Scholar, (c) EBSCOhost, (d) ProQuest, (e) JSTOR, (f) PubMed Central, (g) SAGE, (h) Gale Group, (i) Combined Arms Research Library Catalog, and (j) DTIC. The search terms this research used included (a) *confidence-building measures,* (b) *confidence and security building measures,* (c) *trust building,* and (d) *confidence-building.* The strategy used for identifying historically seminal studies and theorists' writings included tracing back of bibliographical resources from recent articles to articles to original research.

This literature review included consideration of the different authors' definitions of what confidence-building measures are and categorical delineations between types of measures. The most appropriate time interval for current sources was the last five years. However, the use of older publications was critical as the conceptual origins of confidence-building measures go back for decades. To cover the topic fully, and ensure that the literature review was exhaustive, the literature review reaches back to when the term "confidence-building" originated in the 1950s.

The strategy for focusing in on empirical research that most closely resembles the current study was to focus first on where the term originated in the political science and international relation fields. Next, the focus moved to the major approaches of the psychology field. The researcher then focused on the conflict resolution field to determine what current conflict resolution practitioners thought concerning the relevance of confidence-building measures. Finally, the major sources that discussed the foundations of contemporary military operations were explored to evaluate the context fully.

Conceptual Origins

The idea of confidence-building measures originated with Charles Osgood, a popular television announcer (Osgood, 1959, 1962). His idea was relatively simple: If the arms race could gradually escalate through a downward spiral of fear and tension, it could also deescalate in a similar fashion. He believed that if one party announced their intentions and then took a step toward reducing tension then other side could do the same. Eventually this would prevent the unthinkable existential threat from occurring, nuclear war. Osgood labeled this idea GRIT, or graduated reciprocation in tension reduction. Pilisuk and Skolnick (1968) conducted a laboratory experiment that validated the Osgood hypothesis, and their research indicated that the concept had validity in practical application.

Perspectives from the Political Science and International Relations Field

Thirty-five nations signed the United Nations' (1975) Helsinki Declaration which described the purpose of the confidence-building measures in the Declaration "to eliminate the causes of tension that may exist among states and thus of contributing to the strengthening of peace and security in the world" (United Nations, 1975, p. 9). Later, the Tenth Special Session of the United Nations' (1978) General Assembly stated that added confidence-building measures included activities that improved (a) communications, (b) reporting research for military purposes, and (c) other periodic reports. The United Nations Centre for Disarmament Agreement (1982) added an additional measure that called for the signatories to identify areas of disagreement.

Jorgen-Holst (1983) was one of the premier academic writers on the subject of confidence-building measures in the 1980s. He defined confidence-building measures as "arrangement(s) designed to enhance such assurance of mind and belief in the trustworthiness of states and the facts they create" (p. 2). He described the necessity for these measures as the fact that, in general, in international relations, there are only a few formal structures, such as the UN and the World Court, that have power over nations to enforce positive behavior. To him, confidence-building measures are "building blocks that provide operational substance to the notion of common security" (p. 2). Jorgen-Holst categorized confidence-building measures into two classes: (a) those designed to inhibit the political exploitation of the use of force, and (b) those that reduce the chances of a surprise attack.

Schelling (1984) wrote about confidence-building measures and described them as inherently risky, that a party should not risk critical things, and that confidence could backslide at any time. Burt (1984) offered another scholarly view of confidence and trust building measures as additions to or replacements for treaties because formal treaties were notoriously difficult to develop. Overall, he believed that the idea was valid and could help a polarized world avoid nuclear war.

In the mid-1980s, the final agreement of the United Nations' (1986) Stockholm Conference further clarified these measures in the minds of political leaders of the time. The document described confidence-building measures as:

> Effective and concrete actions designed to make progress in strengthening confidence and security and in achieving disarmament, so as to give effect and expression to the duty of states to refrain from the threat or use of force in their mutual relations as well as in their international relations in general. (p.1)

Borawski (1986) presented an excellent academic review of confidence-building measures in the context of the Cold War period as it they relates to nuclear arms control. His model of confidence-building measure employment includes three categories: (a) information exchange, (b) observation and inspection, and (c) operational constraints. In this model, the informational exchange has the purpose of increasing mutual understanding and knowledge to increase the awareness of the difference between actions and deeds. For observation and inspection, the purpose is to allow for an independent assessment of military activities. Finally, operational constraints limit military activities by regulating how, when, and where they can apply confidence-building measures. This model is representative of the general academic opinion of confidence-building measures during the 1980s

Borawski's (1986) discussion delved deep into the history of confidence-building measures suggesting that they have existed for some time in many forms and have been referred to by other terminology. Going back to 1816, he cited that Lord Castlereagh suggested that world powers should provide freely information on current arms stockpiles to dispel alarm. He also discussed the 1930 Greco-Turkish Protocol as an example, where each side agreed to disclose their purchase of new naval vessels six months before purchase. In addition, he has cited President Eisenhower's "Open Skies" proposal where each superpower would allow over flight inspections of their nuclear arsenals. Borawski has argued that the first real confidence-building measure (referred to as such) was the direct communications hotline established between the United States and Soviet Union in 1963 following the Cuban Missile crisis. Throughout the remainder of the 1980s, academics continued to evaluate and discuss the topic of confidence-building measures in the Cold-War context (Gillian, Crawford, & Buczek, 1987; Nation, 1989; Vick, 1988).

United Nations' (1992) Vienna Convention document reinforced the previous document's definition of confidence-building measures word-for-word. In the progression of agreements, from Helsinki, to Stockholm, to Vienna, the concept of confidence-building was refined. As the concept of confidence-building measures further matured, users of confidence-building measures applied the concept in areas not directly related to the Cold War.

Through the 1990s, authors continued to write on the topic. Chevrier (1998) offered a skeptic's view and concluded that they are not a panacea for dealing with difficult issues such as chemical and biological weapons. Singh (1998) discussed measures that China and India had employed, expanding the context of the idea beyond its traditional Cold War context.

The 1990s saw the first use of confidence-building measures in South America. In 1996, members of the Organization of American States (OAS) signed a resolution adopting confidence- and security-building measures in the Americas. The OAS acknowledged the concept of confidence-building measures as valid and decided to employ these measures to help keep the peace and lessen tensions in its sphere of influence. Major provisions included all countries informing the body of military expenditures; notifying the body in advance of military exercises; issuing invitations to observe military exercises; developing means of communication; and holding seminars, courses, and studies (OAS, 1997). Beyond this new application, this period also saw many more scholars writing on the topic of confidence-building measures.

Beginning in 1991, the Stimson Center, a non-profit and non-partisan institution devoted to enhancing security and peace internationally, has acted as a proponent and advocate for confidence-building as an approach to problem solving between nations. Their confidence-building program consists of six primary components: (a) meetings with various stakeholders, (b) academic papers, (c) workshops inside regions of interest, (d) a visiting research fellows program, (e) publication and distribution of printed materials, and (f) posting of materials on their website. Their experience and continual dialogue made the Stimson Center an important piece of the equation needed to understand the full picture of what confidence-building measures are and how they work in a contemporary context (Krepon, McCoy, & Rudolph, 1999).

The Stimson Center has offered some points of discussion that are critical to understanding the context of the topic. Krepon, Newbill, Khoja, and Drezin (1999) asserted that confidence-building measures, although first conceptualized during the Cold War, have applicability beyond just Western countries. They also asserted that taking Western confidence-building measures and applying them as an exact template is not optimal and that parties should consider the unique characteristics of each conflict appropriately. The authors felt that because parties often employ confidence-building measures informally, these measures are easier to implement than formal intergovernmental agreements.

Krepon, Newbill, et al. (1999) suggested a model for confidence-building measures consisting of three phases: (a) conflict avoidance, (b) confidence-building, and (c) reinforcement of the peace. In the first phase, they suggested that conflict-avoidance measures might be the more appropriate term. Overall, the authors believed that confidence-building measure are relevant to keep conflicts from backsliding but that stakeholders directly involved in conflict must have a hand in formulating the solution.

Cossa (as cited in Krepon, Newbill, et al., 1999) has presented a description of the results of an international working group of the Council of Security Cooperation in the Asia-Pacific area. This working group offered a solid operational definition of confidence-building measures as:

> Formal and informal measures, whether unilateral, bilateral, or multilateral that address, prevent, or resolve uncertainties between states, including military and political elements. Such measures contribute to a reduction of uncertainty, misperception, and suspicion and thus help to reduce the possibility of an incidental or accidental war. (p. 27)

This working group also presented numerous conclusions of importance to an overview on the topic of confidence-building measures. First, the concept of confidence-building measures cannot work when all parties are unwilling to cooperate. Second, parties must consider confidence-building as a win-win, not a win-lose proposition. Third, parties must employ confidence-building measures in the context of existing contextual norms. Fourth, measures that worked in one situation and for one country may not work in another situation or with another country. Fifth, parties should view measures as stepping-stones and building blocks, not institutions. Sixth, parties should employ measures that are realistic and pragmatic, and have clearly defined objectives. One of the final points was that parties should employ measures that are gradual and incremental and not seek to achieve too much too quickly.

Many authors continued to explore the various potential contexts of confidence-building including conflict in the Middle East (Emamjomehzadeh & Jahanshahrad, 2003; Rathmell, 2000; Steinberg, 2004), Argentina and Brazil (Higgins, 2001), China and Taiwan (Glaser, 2005), Japan and Russia (Ota, 2009), Pakistan and India, (Hilali, 2005; Kahn, 2010; Raju, 2009) and the general nature of confidence-building measures (Lachowski, 2010; Muniruzzaman, 2010). Of interest to this research, Johnstone and Corbin (2008) argued that military activity helped to build trust. In one of the more interesting studies of the period Gottwald et al. (2009) used the Correlates of War (COW) project, a large body of data collected about war, to analyze the concept of confidence-building measures. Their quantitative results indicated that confidence-building measures did have validity when addressing conflict between two nation states. From the middle of the 20th century into the beginning of the 21st century, the literature indicated that scholars accepted the idea of confidence-building measures in the political science and international relations fields.

Perspectives from the Field of Psychology

In the field of psychology, trust is function of individual choices shaped by environmental (nurture), biological or genetic make-up (nature), and personal choices (free will; Parish & Barness, 2009). It is possible that the field of psychology can offer a valuable academic perspective that can provide a deeper understanding of what makes up the emotional side of confidence and trust and how people build confidence.

The humanistic approach to psychology highlights the human need for safety, empathy, and acceptance (Maslow, 1943; Rogers, 1980). Additionally, Rowan (2001) stated that an encounter is where one party simply treats the other as a human being. When one applies the lens of humanistic psychology to confidence-building measures, one can see that the common confidence-building measures could work because humans all share a need for safety and acceptance. Here, the confidence-building measures become the encounter between individuals, helping them realize the mutual needs and dependence each shares.

The cognitive-behavioral approach to psychology has offered additional insights to trust building applicable to this research. This approach is one of the major cotemporary approaches in the field today and scholar-practitioners apply it across the various sub-fields of psychology. The approach grew out of the behavioral perspective and has proven effective in treating many psychological pathologies (Carter, Forys, & Oswald, 2008). In contemporary practice, cognitive behavioral therapy explores how the mind conceptualizes situations, assigns meaning to them, and guides behavioral response to those situations. At its core, cognitive therapy uses probing questions to help stimulate other viewpoints in a process of guided discovery. This helps people become more aware of how they think and helps them understand the meanings that come to mind in certain situations. The therapeutic methods used target symptoms, help others re-evaluate thought processes, and promote helpful behavioral responses (British Association for Behavioural and Cognitive Psychotherapies, 2011).

Wright et al. (2006) have presented a basic cognitive-behavioral model in which a person iteratively goes through the stages of (a) event; (b) cognitive appraisal (including automatic thoughts); (c) emotion; and, finally, (d) behavior. Through restructuring the subject's cognitive appraisal, the cognitive behavioral approach seeks to influence the resulting behavior. This has interesting implications for the concept of confidence-building.

In a conflict, those involved interpret events and actions taken by the other party and then behave in a manner they feel is appropriate to the situation, given their cognitive understanding.

Confidence-building works in the cognitive appraisal part of the cycle, and, as such, can lead to the interpretation of events in a different manner than the parties may have interpreted them in the past. This is important for numerous reasons. One can interpret almost any event in a positive or negative way, depending on the frame, perspective, and point of view. If parties have successfully used a confidence-building measure in the past, it could lead to a different cognitive interpretation. With a different cognitive interpretation comes a different emotional reaction, and, possibly, a different response. Much like a therapy client who is trying to restructure his or her thoughts when craving drugs, confidence-building measures restructure the thoughts of parties in conflict. Instead of one party assuming negative intent with every action, the idea that the other party may not intend damage lessens the chance of negative interpretation. Simply put, if one can analyze the cognitive processes of the mind, as cognitive-behaviorists assert, confidence-building measures represent a restructuring of thought in a positive direction.

From the bio-psychological view, trust is chemical and physical responses to stimuli. Kruger et al. (2007) found that during negotiation, the paracingular cortex and the septal area were the areas of the brain most stimulated, and, when people made the decision to trust, the paracingular cortex in the brain is activated. They concluded that these brain structures stimulate the release of the neuropeptides oxytocin and vasopressin to affect social learning. Interestingly, even if the oxytocin is artificial it can induce trust in strangers. This trust bond, once formed, is difficult to reverse (Evans et al., 2011).

Dimoka (2010) used fMRI technology to investigate the trust phenomena. He found that the neural correlates of trust were (a) the caudate nucleus, (b) the putamen, (c) the anterior paracingulate cortex, and (d) orbitofrontal cortex. For distrust, the neural correlates were the amygdala and insular cortex, commonly linked with negative emotions, such as fear and loss. Bosa, Terburga, and van Honka (2010) conducted research that concluded testosterone also decreased trust between individuals. Figure 1 depicts a summary of findings from biopsychological research on trust in three states: (a) full trust, (b) conditional trust, and (c) distrust.

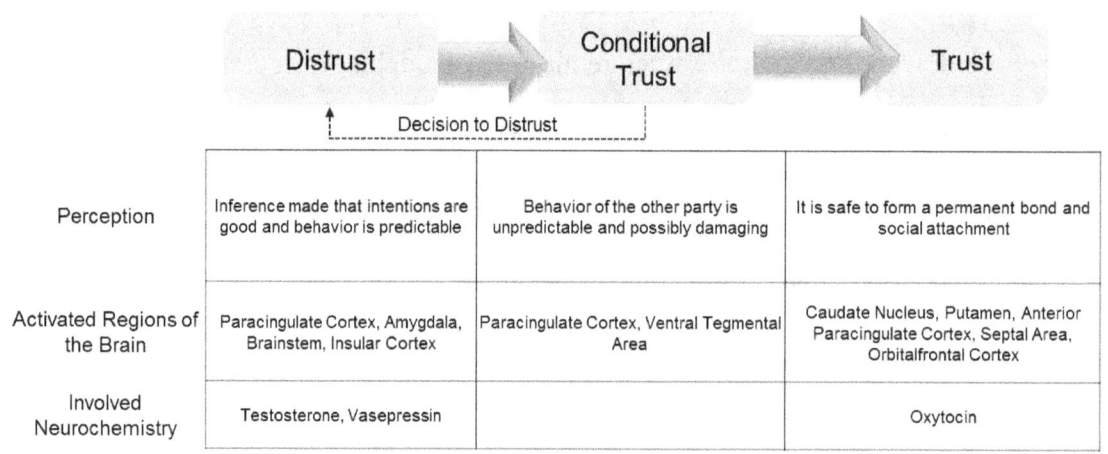

Figure 1. Summary of bio-psychological research on trust.

Costa (2003) has described the perspective of the applied psychology sub-field on trust and asserted that, in general, there are two types of trust, interpersonal and institutional. Costa has asserted that the topic of trust has enjoyed increased attention because of its importance in the organizational context and has described the many definitions of trust in contemporary use. First, applied psychology views trust as either a psychological state or behavioral choice based on expectations of another party's behavior. What is valuable to this research is the idea that trust is a choice behavior, and hence, conditionally based. However, Costa also acknowledged that trust is highly complex and contains components of cognition, emotion, and behavior founded in experiences and an assessment of the behavior of others as a careful calculation of risk and reward.

Interesting to this research is Costa's (2003) description of an individual personal predisposition to trust where people generally give others the benefit of the doubt until they prove themselves as untrustworthy. On the topic of how one can develop trust with another, Costa identifies three major models: (a) calculus-based trust, (b) knowledge-based trust, and (c) identification-based trust. Table 1 depicts the characteristics of the three models.

Table 1

Trust Models

Title	Description	How Trust is Built
Calculus-based	Calculation of benefits and threat	Making agreements, establishing the rules, monitoring and predictability
Knowledge-based	Having ample information to predict the others behavior	Regular communication and interaction
Identification-based	Identification with the other's desires and intentions	Showing empathy, sharing needs, choices, and preferences

These three models from the field of applied psychology have numerous insights for this research on confidence-building. First, there is an apparent progression implied from one type of trust to the next. In calculus-based trust, it comes from the aspect of conditionality and predictability. As more knowledge about each other develops, the parties in conflict understand the behavior and finally identify with each other through a common identity. Second, although these models do not mention confidence-building measures directly, one can infer that these models describe why communication is central to confidence-building.

Perspectives from the Conflict Resolution Field

Three primary sources have discussed the use of confidence-building measures in the context of the conflict resolution field. Landau and Landau (1997) discussed that in mediation these measures may have validity and that measures in mediation should include unconditional and unilateral gestures. They stated that at the beginning of a mediation, session parties could use gestures to establish good will and set a positive tone and communicate a willingness to consider the other's needs. Second, Furlong (2005) described the tendency of a party in conflict to attribute negative events to the other party in the conflict, and that confidence-building measures can serve to reduce this tendency. He outlined a two-step process of confidence-building that included creation of a safe environment and then implementation of confidence-building measures.

Finally, Sandole et al. (2009) compiled and edited a comprehensive account of other authors that provide significant intellectual depth on the application of confidence-building measures. Kelman (2009) argued that building trust is a form of mutual reassurance. Woolford and Ratner (2009) argued that confidence-building measures work in the mediation room as well. Overall, the literature indicated the use of confidence-building measures as an acknowledged part of the academic dialogue.

Narrowing the Context: The U.S. Military's Operational Environment

To construct a theoretical model for practical use by the U.S. military, it is critical to explore the context of military doctrine and key concepts. The Department of Defense's (2012) *Capstone Concept for Joint Operations* is the document that sits at the apex of U.S. military joint doctrine and describes what the joint force does and how it will accomplish its mission. The U.S. military is one of the many instruments of national power that policymakers can employ to protect and further national interests. The concept describes the ten primary missions for military forces as (a) counter terrorism and irregular warfare, (b) deter and defeat aggression, (c) project power, (d) counter weapons of mass destruction, (e) operate effectively in cyberspace and outer space, (f) maintain a nuclear deterrent, (g) defend the homeland, (h) provide stabilizing presence, (i) conduct stability and counter insurgency operations, and (j) conduct humanitarian disaster relief and other operations. Inherent within the vast majority of these potential missions is that service members will operate with various host nation stakeholders to further the strategic ends of the nation.

Each unique situation that the U.S. military faces comes with its own challenges. Joint doctrine refers to the environment in which these operations take place as the operational environment. The joint community defined the operational environment as "a composite of the conditions, circumstances, and influences that affect the employment of capabilities and bear on the decisions of the commander" (Department of Defense, 2011, p. GL-14). One major assumption that joint doctrine made is that within the operational environment, political leadership will ask the military to perform its duties in environments of uncertainty, complexity, rapid change, and persistent conflict. Within the operational environment, military commanders employ forces in a joint operational area, defined as "an area of land, sea, and airspace, defined by a geographic combatant commander or subordinate unified commander, in which a joint force commander (normally a joint task force commander) conducts military operations to accomplish a specific mission" (Department of Defense, 2011, p. GL-12). Within the physical boundaries of this area, units and individuals will likely encounter civilians either purposefully or because of other assigned tasks.

Joint doctrine fully acknowledges the importance that interaction with civilians has for successful mission execution and defines civil-military operations as:

> The activities of a commander that establish, maintain, influence, or exploit relations between military forces, governmental and nongovernmental civilian organizations and authorities, and the civilian populace in a friendly, neutral, or hostile operational area in order to facilitate military operations, to consolidate and achieve operational U.S. objectives. Civil-military operations may include performance by military forces of activities and functions normally the responsibility of the local, regional, or national government. These activities may occur prior to, during, or subsequent to other military actions. They may also occur, if directed, in the absence of other military operations. Designated civil affairs forces, other military forces, or by a

combination of civil affairs and other forces can conduct civil military operations (Department of Defense, 2008, p. GL-6).

In addition to interacting with civilian populations, U.S. military forces often ask service members to interact, train, and cooperate with members of foreign militaries. Joint doctrine refers to this as military engagement, defined as:

> Routine contact and interaction between individuals or elements of the Armed Forces of the United States and those of another nation's armed forces, or foreign and domestic civilian authorities or agencies to build trust and confidence, share information, coordinate mutual activities, and maintain influence. (Department of Defense, 2011, GL-13)

These definitions outline three major categories of stakeholders that the military asks service members to interact with in the conduct of their missions within the operational environment: (a) civilians, (b) militaries of other nations, and (c) foreign and domestic civilian authorities or agencies. It is also important to note that joint doctrine specifically addresses the importance of building confidence with these populations. In the conduct of joint operations, the military can use confidence-building measures to gain an operational advantage. If political leaders can employ confidence-building at the macro level, it can also have benefits at the micro level.

When forward deployed, the U.S. military asks soldiers, sailors, airmen, and marines, at all levels to perform in positions where they must successfully interact with local populations. This interaction can come in the form of sitting down with a tribal leader in a small village in Afghanistan or acting as a military liaison at an embassy, conducting multi-lateral counter-piracy operations, or enforcing a no-fly zone with a fighter jet of another nation. Even though conceptually the literature indicated that confidence-building measures work to improve the interactions of nations at the strategic level, the military could apply the methodology to just about any interaction with foreign civilians or military members.

Privates, sergeants, and lieutenants could benefit from the application of confidence-building measures as much as generals, ambassadors, or heads-of-state.

Relevant Military Publications

The Commandant of the Marine Corps, General Charles Krulack (1999) drafted an article that described the service member of the future and the skills and attributes that they would require. At the time he wrote, he had no way of predicting the events that would lead to America's deployment of forces into Iraq and Afghanistan. However, his article described the criticality of what he calls the "strategic corporal," or an individual service member with disproportionally large strategic affect. For this research, this article provided the insight into just how important small interactions are in resolving complex circumstances. It also highlighted that often the roles service members perform do not deal directly with conflict.

The most recent version of the U.S. Army's (2006) *Counterinsurgency Manual* has proven instrumental in crystallizing military thought on counterinsurgent operations in Iraq and Afghanistan and describing the importance of building confidence between the U.S. military and civilians, local military and police forces, and U.S. and host nation interagency stakeholders. The center of gravity for any military operation is considered as the source of power for a military force. The center of gravity for a counterinsurgency operation is often "the ability to generate and sustain popular support, or at least acquiescence and tolerance" (U.S. Army, 2006, pp. 3-13). This manual stated that if a local government can provide basic security, it can then gain confidence and legitimacy in other areas. Time is also an important component in stimulating the confidence of the populace, with a necessity for the population to believe in the staying power and resilience of the local government and security forces.

In addition, if military or police operations abuse civilians in any way, this serves to degrade confidence and possibly fuel support for the insurgents. After the military trains and employs police or military forces, if these forces fail or are corrupt, the population could also lose trust in them and look to the opposition and not to the local government for guidance and governance. For success in counterinsurgency operations, unit commanders must use patience, presence, and courage to increase the confidence level among the local civilians while defeating insurgent forces and decreasing the insurgent's legitimacy. In summary, the importance of building confidence with the civilian population and host nation is a consistent theme throughout contemporary counterinsurgency doctrine (U.S. Army, 2006).

The Center for Army Lessons Learned (CALL) publishes numerous documents that take soldier experiences and draft different products to help them apply best practices and lessons learned. They have numerous publications available that address the importance of relationships of service members with indigenous personnel and are of interest to this research. CALL (2010) suggested that Provincial Reconstruction Teams encourage local governance by pursuing (a) legitimacy of and trust in state institutions, (b) political will and committed leadership, (c) security, (d) delivering basic services, (e) rule of law, (f) transparency and accountability, and (g) a civil society. Relationships are important within the conceptual frameworks that CALL describes.

McKavitt (2013) offered advice to potential advisors in Afghanistan that address topics related to confidence-building. His list offered one service member's experience in advising border police. Among his key points, he emphasized the importance of (a) rapport, (b) spending time with those you advise, and (c) speaking openly. Although this article did not mention confidence-building measures directly, the author's view has validity and offers a perspective of interest to this research.

The literature surveyed during the literature review set the stage for the conduct of this study. The existing literature is rich in discussion of confidence and trust building measures from the perspectives of the international relations, political science, and psychology fields. As one could reasonably expect, each of these field utilized its own methods to draw conclusions for those seeking to build confidence during conflict. There were no sources identified that investigated the application of confidence-building measures in the context of soldiers deployed in a contemporary context. Therefore, the exploratory nature of theory development, specifically, the grounded theory method of qualitative research, was a prudent way for this research to develop an initial understanding into the unique nature of confidence-building measures and how confidence-building was applied, either purposefully or out of necessity, in the challenging and complex environments of Iraq and Afghanistan.

CHAPTER 3: METHOD

This chapter describes the methodology that was used to collect data and describe the phenomenon of confidence-building measures in the contemporary joint environment. This chapter provides the overarching framework for the conduct of the research in the field and covers the specifics of the qualitative methodology selected, the study participants, data collection, procedures followed, trustworthiness, ethical concerns, and data analysis. Specifically, to address the problem statement, this chapter will describe the details of how the researcher constructed a theoretical model of how U.S. service members employ confidence-building measures to build trust over time with key stakeholders in the contemporary joint operational environment.

Overall, a qualitative approach using a grounded theory methodology was employed in five phases: (a) research initiation, (b) theoretical model creation, (c) literature review triangulation, (d) subject matter expert triangulation, and (e) research conclusion (see Figure 2). This approach was best suited to this research because the ultimate goal of this research was to create a usable theoretical model that uses inductive logic to describe human emotion and behavior validated by those who employed the methodologies investigated in this study.

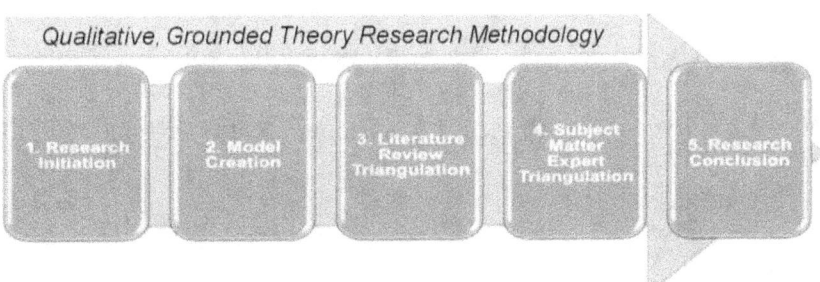

Figure 2. Research design.

Methodology Selected

The researcher employed a qualitative research design and, more specifically, utilized a grounded theory approach to develop a theoretical model of confidence-building measure employment. Creswell (2004) defined grounded theory research design as "a systematic, qualitative procedure used to generate a theory that explains, at a broad conceptual level, a process, an action, or interaction about a substantive topic" (p. 13).

There are many reasons that the qualitative approach was well suited to address this research problem. Burns and Grove (2010) described the positive attributes of this approach, and when one applies these attributes to this specific research, they highlighted just why this approach was well suited. First, this approach to research is best suited for use when one seeks to understand human emotions, as was the case in this research with the dimensions of trust. Second, because human emotions are difficult to quantify, qualitative research was better suited to investigate emotional responses with no numerical component. Third, because this research sought a holistic understanding, the use of this methodology was advantageous. Fourth, because the qualitative methodology allowed theoretical implications to emerge from the data, it increased the validity of the findings to the real world. Overall, the qualitative approach was best suited to this research because the ultimate goal of the research was to create a theoretical model that uses inductive logic to create an archetype of human emotion and behavior. When researchers use the grounded theory model, their intended purpose is to accomplish theoretical model creation grounded in data from real life events and perceptions.

The grounded theory method is well suited to derive a theory inductively from relevant events and perceptions of behavior systematically as a holistic approach to phenomenology (Egan, 2002; Henwood & Pidgeon, 2003; Simmons, 2011). This approach asserts that a researcher should consider all information as data, with the goal of discovering what phenomena are actually occurring (Glaser, 2001). Creswell (2004) described the many reasons that a researcher would choose a grounded theory design including: (a) to generate a new theory, (b) to explain a process, action, or interaction, (c) when a researcher desires a systematic procedure, and (d) when a researcher wants to get close to the data. All of these reasons were applicable to the goals of this research, and, as such, the grounded theory methodology was an excellent fit.

In the initial stages of this project, the researcher explored other design methodologies for suitability. Since the driving goal of this research was to create a new theoretical model, not simply expand upon an accepted theoretical model, the researcher ruled out the quantitative approach. In addition, trying to quantify the experiences of building trust would have been very difficult because one person's high level of trust may not be another's. These potential differences in personal perception scale also led the researcher to rule out the quantitative approach.

The specific research question for this inquiry was, "What is a theory, grounded in the data, that explains how U.S. service members apply confidence building measures to build trust with key indigenous stakeholders in the contemporary joint operational environment?"

Service members who had suitable experience in the field building confidence with indigenous stakeholders were identified and their informed consent was gained. Data were collected, analyzed, and synthesized into a theoretical model. The research followed a grounded theory methodology with triangulation against the literature review and subsequently with subject matter experts. In the interest of full disclosure, during this research, the researcher was serving in the military and has, in the past, served in positions where he has been required to build trust with host nation militaries and civilians. However, the author's experience was in Pakistan, not in Afghanistan or Iraq. Therefore, while the researcher's interest and experience led to the current research, the context of the problem is outside of the primary researcher's experience set.

Bracketing techniques were applied to attempt to eliminate researcher bias, a problem common with qualitative research. Patton (1990) stated that the goal of research is to describe the essence of what and how people experience. This essence is composed of the commonalities of the human experience. Another key factor is epoche, where a researcher eliminates prejudices and assumptions and investigates the phenomenon in a clear and unobstructed manner. Researchers commonly accomplish this through phenomenological reduction (bracketing) to prevent extraneous intrusions of obfuscating data.

Patton (1990) recommended that to avoid biases, researchers should conduct bracketing by (a) locating key phases that speak directly to the phenomena, (b) interpreting the meanings of these phrases, (c) analyzing these recurring features of the phenomenon, (d) re-defining the phenomenon, (e) portraying each theme, and (d) developing a structural synthesis. During coding of the data, these areas of focus were sequentially applied to approach the data in an open and unbiased manner. The coding itself followed this method of bracketing to approach the data in an open manner that other scholars could reproduce if needed.

Study Participants

In a grounded theory approach to research, researchers use purposive theoretical sampling over representative or random sampling (Glaser, 1998). At the time of the study, for the first time since the Vietnam War, the United States military had a tremendous wealth of recent and relevant combat experience building confidence among multiple stakeholders. From 2002 to 2012, there were an estimated 1,425,200 service member deployments to Iraq and Afghanistan, with many service members having deployed multiple times (Belasco, 2009). Although the individual roles and experiences of each service member vary, the nature of counterinsurgency operations in Iraq and Afghanistan created the necessity of service members to adapt ways to build confidence with local populations, indigenous security forces, and other partners.

Not all service members will have served in positions in which they were required to build trust, and based on their rank, they may have worked with host-nation civilians or militaries in different contexts. Instead of attempting to capture every experience, if there are true commonalities upon which to base a theory, these themes will emerge from a small number of in-depth accounts. This is one of the key tenets of the grounded theory approach to research (Glaser, 2001).

Small, but in-depth qualitative interviews of approximately one hour in duration and focused on quality over quantity characterize the grounded theory approach. Rather than use a strict percentage of sample size, Strauss and Corbin (1998) stated that in the grounded theory approach, data saturation is the goal. Data saturation occurs when (a) no new or relevant data emerges, (b) the categories in the theoretical model are well defined, and (c) the relationships between categories are established. This point of saturation is unknowable before the research begins and will vary based on the scope of the research topic.

To focus the data collection on the right sample with the right experience set, the researcher identified the sample through an existing database of in-depth service member interviews to identify those with the most recent and relevant experience. Permission was granted to use the archive of interviews held by the U.S. Army's Operational Leadership Experiences Database (see Appendix A). This open-source database is an oral history project that collects, transcribes, and makes available personal experiences of service members and civilians who have had firsthand deployment experience since September 11, 2001. This included those who have directly participated in, planned, or supported operations relevant to confidence-building. The U.S. Army Combat Studies Institute oversees the training of interviewers and the collection of data and makes transcribed interviews available to the public. The transcripts provided names of participants, dates of data collection, location of data collection, and, in some cases, the raw video or audio of the interview. This database provided all transcripts formatted uniformly in a .pdf format (CSI, 2012).

At the time of the research, the database included 2,515 interview transcripts in a searchable format. To capture data relevant to the desired subject matter and sample, the researcher used key search terms, in the Boolean full-text search engine, to narrow the scope to the most relevant personal accounts. The first search delimiting terms used were "confidence" or "trust." This search returned 776 interview results. The delimiter placed search conducted was one that searched for all interviews collected after 2008. This narrowed the results to 279. However, the provided search feature only allows one to search for the date the interviewer questioned the interviewee, not the date of actual deployment experience. Thus, the 279 results were screened manually to ensure the subjects' experience date fell within the five-year parameters of 2008 to 2012.

The researcher identified 123 interviews that provided accounts of deployment experiences since 2008. Each interview was manually reviewed for relevance to the desired context of working with indigenous stakeholders. For example, if the word "trust" or "confidence" is used in the context with an interviewee's fellow soldiers, then it would not meet the screening criteria, and the interview was excluded from the study. Based on the initial in-depth review of these interviews, 67 interviews met the screening criteria. The researcher then uploaded the identified reviews into the NVivo software platform and data was coded to create the initial theoretical model.

During data coding, interviewees with the most relevant recent experience were identified as subject matter experts for subsequent theoretical model verification. The researcher used the grounded theory approach technique of purposive sampling to narrow the scope to those few who had the most experience with the phenomena of building trust. This methodology was advantageous because those who had the richest and most in-depth experiences with the phenomenon were those from which the theoretical model is constructed and ultimately triangulated. The ultimate goal was to obtain the richest data possible concerning the phenomenon through progressively honing in on those subjects with the most relevant recent experience.

The screening criteria that each subject matter expert met were (a) an interviewee whose primary duties included regular interaction with indigenous stakeholders, (b) an interviewee who described more than one instance of confidence-building measure use, and (c) an interviewee identified as having more than one deployment to Iraq or Afghanistan. Before beginning the research and screening the interviews, the exact number of subject matter experts that the data would yield was difficult to determine; however, the goal is a minimum of 10% of the contextually relevant interviews.

The number of experts identified was 27. Of these, the researcher was able to verify

24 email addresses by searching public databases. The researcher contacted each expert and asked him to volunteer for an in-depth interview. Ten experts volunteered to participate in follow-on interviews for this study. Following this, in-depth interviews were conducted with the subject matter expert sample to triangulate, validate, and further refine the derived theoretical model (see Figure 3). Research has indicated that grounded theory studies range from 4 to 82 subjects (Mason, 2010), and the number of subjects for this research fell within that range.

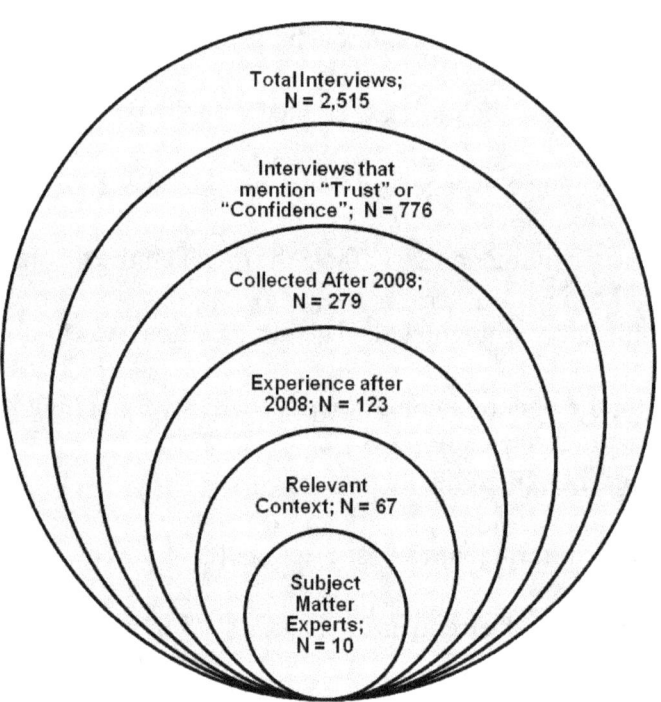

Figure 3. Venn diagram depicting the sample.

Data Collection

The researcher collected data from two qualitative sources. An existing collection of in-depth service member interviews was used to develop the initial theoretical model as described above. All transcript files that fit the screening criteria were downloaded from the

Operational Leadership Project Database to a personal computer. Next, open coding was conducted to screen context of search results to ensure that only the data that fit within the context of building confidence and trust with indigenous stakeholders in Iraq and Afghanistan. Finally, all transcript files were uploaded to the NVivo qualitative data analysis platform.

In the second part of data collection, the researcher collected data through subsequent original interviews with subject matter experts. Email addresses of the subject matter experts were obtained, and the potential experts were sent an email message asking for their voluntary participation and completion of the informed consent (see Appendices B and D). Upon receipt of the informed consent form, the researcher set up a meeting time and conducted an interview in person, via telephone, or via video teleconference with each volunteer according to the interview guide (see Appendix C). Finally, the files of each transcribed interview were uploaded into the NVivo program for analysis.

Procedures Followed

Overall, the researcher proceeded in five phases: (a) research initiation, (b) theoretical model creation, (c) literature review triangulation, (d) subject matter expert triangulation, and (e) research conclusion. The specific elements of each phase are as follows:

Phase 1: Research Initiation.

1. Submitted proposal to the Institutional Review Board (IRB) for approval and adjustment as required.

2. Began data collection once the IRB had granted permission to proceed.

Phase 2: Theoretical model Creation.

1. Conducted memoing throughout to connect concepts and key ideas that helped formulate the theory at the conclusion of the study.

2. Verified previous search results from the Operational Leadership Experiences Database (full text search terms are "trust" or "confidence" and delimited to only those collected after 2008).

3. Screened search results to ensure the subjects' experience dates fell within the five-year parameters of 2008-2012.

4. Downloaded all transcript files from the Operational Leadership Project Database that fit the screening criteria to a personal computer.

5. Conducted open coding to screen the context of search results to ensure that only the data that fit within the context of building confidence and trust with indigenous stakeholders in Iraq and Afghanistan.

6. Uploaded all transcript files to the NVivo qualitative data analysis platform.

7. Conducted theoretical coding of data using NVivo software with memoing throughout to connect concepts and key ideas that will help formulate the theory at the conclusion of the study. This step of the research put special emphasis on the causes, contexts, contingencies, consequences, co-variance, and conditions that emerged from the data.

8. Analyzed each transcript line-by-line, paying detailed attention to occurrences of the words "trust" and "confidence" and other key variables that coincided with these statements.

9. Explored the data by manually reviewing each occurrence of the term in context to identify and group types of confidence-building measures applied, and to identify and code other variables that emerge. Specifically, the bracketing was used during coding by:

   a. Locating key phases that speak directly to the central phenomena of trust.

   b. Interpreting the meanings of these phrases.

   c. Analyzing these recurring features of the phenomenon.

   d. Re-defining the phenomenon.

   e. Portraying each theme.

   f. Developing a structural synthesis.

10. During coding, identified subject matter experts for later use for theoretical model verification. The criteria that a subject matter expert met were:

a. An interviewee whose primary duties included regular interaction with indigenous stakeholders.

b. An interviewee who described more than one instance of confidence measure use.

c. An interviewee identified as having more than one deployment to Iraq or Afghanistan.

11. Sorted and developed a theoretical outline connecting the data into a comprehensive theoretical model.

12. Consolidated findings into version one of the theoretical model in NVivo.

Phase 3: Literature Review Triangulation.

1. Uploaded the text of the literature review into the NVivo program.

2. Used NVivo software to code and triangulate the literature review findings with the theoretical model, and conducted memoing throughout (using bracketing methodology described above).

3. Refined the theoretical model through comparing and contrasting the theoretical model with the key lessons and insights summarized from the literature review. The goal of this analysis was to identify how the theoretical model developed from the existing interviews fit within the established body of knowledge on the topic of confidence-building measures. This step ensured that the context of the theoretical model was all inclusive of major thoughts and attitudes of relevant scholars.

4. Consolidated findings into a refined version of the theoretical model in NVivo.

5. Constructed the theoretical model in PowerPoint. The purpose was to create an easy to understand diagram to show to the verification subjects that depicted the central phenomena of confidence-building measure employment and all other identified variables and their relationships to the central phenomena of trust.

Phase 4: Subject Matter Expert Triangulation.

1. Through searching military email databases, Google, Linked-in, and Facebook, determined email addresses of the subject matter experts.

2. Emailed potential experts asking for their voluntary participation. Requested that consenting individuals complete the informed consent form and return it via email (See Appendices A and B).

3. Upon receipt of the informed consent form, set up a meeting time, and conducted an interview either in-person (preferred), via telephone, or via Skype with each volunteer according to the interview guide (See Appendix C). Each interview was recorded.

4. Uploaded the audio file of each interview into the NVivo program.

5. Coded respondents' observations and adjust the theoretical model based on the perceptions of the respondents (using bracketing methodology described above).

Phase 5: Research Conclusion.

1. Made the final adjustments to the theoretical model and developed final chapters of the dissertation.

2. Stored all data within the NVivo program for verification.

3. After five years, destroy all data and physical data storage devices used for data collection.

Trustworthiness and Transferability

Validity of research refers to the fit between the reality of the phenomenon studied, the data, and the findings. The first facet of validity is internal validity or whether the findings fit the subjects' lives and beliefs. The second facet is external validity or whether the findings fit other wider populations in the real world. Inductive logic underlies the grounded theory approach, which, because it uses a small in-depth sample, will have strong internal validity at the cost of external validity. Simply, it reflects the experiences of a few very well at the expense of applicability to a wider population (Sutton & David, 2004).

Barbour (2001) discussed the issues with validity in qualitative research and offered recommendations for how researchers can address these concerns. First, Barbour recommended the use of purposeful sampling where researchers carefully select subjects to ensure they have the experiences upon which to draw quality observations. In this research, a purposive sample was used to ensure the subjects have experience building confidence with host nation civilians or military forces to ensure this research captures observations from the right subjects with real experience.

Second, Barbour (2001) argued that the use of grounded theory method leads to strong internal validity because the research derives theory from data rather than try to prove or disprove a preconceived theory. This is another strong argument for the use of the grounded theory method in this research. Third, Barbour addressed the topic of triangulation, the use of more than one type of data, to increase validity. For this study, the researcher used the literature review to triangulate the concepts of the theory developed and to compare and contrast the findings generated during the research and those generated during the literature review. This was done to strengthen the model and allow for increased external validity.

According to Trochim (2006), the critical aspect of external validity is the ability of the research to generalize the findings to a greater population. External validity relates to the ability of the research propositions, inferences, and conclusions to hold true in other situations. To Trochim, researchers encounter these problems when making connections between the sample taken and with people, places, or times for which the results of the study. First, because the results of this study were generalized for future service members in deployed situations, drawing the sample from current service members maximized external validity in terms of people.

The results from this study are most relevant to U.S. service members and could lose validity when applied to populations of other militaries. Second, in terms of place, the military will continue to deploy service members to Afghanistan through 2014; therefore, the service members could apply these measures there directly. However, a threat to place generalization is that some experiences the researcher drew from included some in Iraq which may not prove directly applicable to future deployments to Afghanistan. Another risk to external validity concerning place is that in the future the military could deploy service members to numerous other locations outside of Iraq and Afghanistan, and the military may ask them to perform different duties, thus changing the context.

This change in context limits the ability to generalize the findings from this study to other places and limits external validity. In terms of the third aspect, time, these findings are the most relevant and generalizable closer to the actual time that the research is conducted. As time passes, these results could represent actual conditions in the field less and less. This would necessitate further studies periodically to provide recent and relevant data for future theoretical model refinement and validation.

Mayring (2011) has presented a thorough discussion of the different aspects of generalization in qualitative research. Mayring argued that generalization in social science research performs the function of (a) inferring general formulations and scientific laws from specific facts; (b) extending the validity of formulations; (c) transferring assumptions over persons, situations, or contexts; and; (d) raising the level of abstraction. The process of generalization works inductively through three major steps including (a) making specific observations, (b) making a theory, and (c) applying the theory to new situation. Mayring argued that researchers accomplish generalization during qualitative research by (a) analysis of total sample, (b) falsification, (c) random or stratified samples, (d) argumentative generalization, (e) theoretical sampling, (f) variation, and (g) triangulation. Based on the type of qualitative research, Mayring believed that use one or more of these methods can help increase the generalizability.

The researcher sought to determine indications of conclusions generalized from specific observations grained through theoretical sampling, variation, and triangulation of the theoretical model with both the literature and subject matter experts. Additionally, since this research sought to collect from two different experience sets (service members with deployments to different locations in Afghanistan and Iraq), there is variation applied that increased the generalization of the data.

Because this research sought a theoretical model for use by future service members in the joint operational environment, this was the primary area in which this research sought to generalize the results. The underlying assumption here was that the theoretical model can transcend specific contextual details and future service members can prudently apply the theoretical model in other countries or regions. To apply this theoretical model effectively in the future, the service members must apply key elements of context, such as (a) cultural considerations, (b) the specific military mission set, and (c) their own personal factors.

First, a measure that builds confidence in one culture could act in an opposite different manner in a culture with different underlying norms and values. The more differences that exist between the cultures of the country where the theoretical model is applied and the cultures of Iraq and Afghanistan, the less useful the service member will find the theoretical model. For example, a soldier deployed to a country in Latin America may find that a local civilian is offended when the soldier applies a confidence-building measure that worked with an Iraqi civilian. Second, the more the mission differs from the counterinsurgency mission that service members faced in Iraq and Afghanistan, the less that users of the theoretical model will find it applicable. For example, if the military deploys a service member to a humanitarian relief mission in Haiti, that mission may call for a different set of measures than what worked during a counterinsurgency mission. Finally, the service member's own personal biases, training, and intuition may make a measure successful or successful. For example, if a service member executes a confidence-building measure poorly, it could cause a lack of confidence in the end. Overall, no theory is without its flaws, and even though this research uses theoretical sampling, variation, and triangulation to increase valid generalization, contextual factors are critical to successful application in the future.

Ethical Concerns

As with any research, with this study the researcher was responsible for protecting the confidentiality of the participants. Confidentiality is an obligation of any research, and the reasonable actions were taken to protect information and safeguard data obtained in accordance with the law and applicable institutional rules. Numerous APA (2012) guidelines are applicable to this research. There is an obligation to obtain only confidential information that is germane to the purpose of the research, and researchers must always obtain institutional approval. Most important for this research endeavor was the need to obtain informed consent from the participants to conduct this research.

At the time of the research, the OLE database listed ranks and full names of the interview participants. Even though the researcher used this database to identify subjects for further study, the researcher did not record or report findings that further identify subject matter experts by name and rank. The research only identified subject matter expert interviewees by a reference number and not by name, rank, or any other recognizable biographical characteristics.

To address the APA (2012) requirements, no information was sought that was not germane to the research. Only minimal biographical data was collected from the participants and no social security numbers, addresses, or any other information that other parties could use to compromise financial data or defraud the participants. For the requirement of confidentiality during creating, storing, accessing, and transferring of records, due diligence was maintained by establishing a password for data files and adequately securing computer hardware upon which the information is stored. The researcher obtained institutional approval through the dissertation committee and the University of Rockies Institutional Review Board. Finally, this study incorporated an informed consent disclaimer to ensure the researcher made the subject aware of the ethical guidelines employed. Research participants agreed to the terms and conditions of the informed consent statement. If the participants did not agree to the disclaimer, the researcher did not conduct an interview with that person. All data was saved in digital format, and stored files were encrypted and password protected on an external hard drive. No data files were uploaded onto the public Internet. The researcher will keep the data for a period of five years, then erase the data and physically destroy the external drive.

The goals of this research were purely academic in nature, and, as such, the University of the Rockies Institutional Review Board provided requisite oversight. The researcher complied with all applicable procedures and reviews accordingly before, during, and after data collection. The researcher did not seek to determine any official U.S. government position and considered all volunteers as individuals making personal statements concerning their own experiences.

The researcher did not represent the study as an official U.S. government research project and did not represent any accounts or conclusions to the U.S. military as a whole or in part as an official government position. The researcher did not conduct interviews on any U.S. government installation or using any government facilities or resources. The researcher only used interviews that reflect personal experience and accounts of trust-building. The U.S. Army's Combat Studies Institute has granted permission for the researcher to use the Operational Leadership Experiences Database (see Appendix A).

The researcher did not collect any information that one could consider confidential or proprietary. Additionally, the researcher did not pull from any sources that the government would consider classified or that otherwise threatened national security, such as specific locations, names, or other information that could jeopardize ongoing operations. Study participants were instructed not to disclose any information of a classified nature or any information that would threaten loss of information regarding intelligence collection methods and procedures. The informed consent form was reviewed with the participants before the study began and emphasis was placed on the unclassified nature of the discussion. Additionally, if participants disclosed any such information inadvertently or the discussion began to go into specifics that included locations, other people, or ongoing operations, the researcher removed the records of that information to prevent any further inappropriate information exposure.

Data Analysis

Henwood and Pidgeon (2003) described the phases of grounded theory research as follows:

1. Open-coding to capture the detail, variation, and complexity of the basic qualitative material (sometimes also referred to as substantive coding);

2a. Constantly comparing data instances, cases, and categories for conceptual similarities and differences (the method of constant comparison);

2b. Sampling new data and cases on theoretical grounds as analysis progresses (theoretical sampling to extend the emergent theory by checking out emerging ideas, extending richness and scope, and in particular to add qualitative variety to the core data included within the analysis;

2c. Writing theoretical memoranda to explore emerging concepts and links to existing theory;

3a. Engaging in more focused coding (including focused, axial, and theoretical coding) of selected core categories;

3b. Continuing to code, make comparisons, and sample theoretically until the point at which no new relevant insights are being reached (theoretical saturation); and,

4. Additional tactics to move analysis from descriptive to levels that are more theoretical, for example, grouping or reclassifying sets of basic categories; writing definitions of core categories; building conceptual models and data displays; linking to the existing literature; writing extended memos and more formal theory (Henwood & Pidgeon, 2003, p. 136).

Grounded theory methodology was used to analyze the data, where all information is data. Even though this study began with a comprehensive literature review, data was investigated independent of this theoretical model, combining and synthesizing a completed theoretical model only at the end of the research. A constant comparative analysis involved a continual process of collecting, coding, and analyzing the data to identify categories that reveal themselves. The researcher coded and analyzed the data simultaneously along with memo writing to ensure the research captured observations as soon as the researcher made them (Bailey, 2010).

Specifically, coding of the data was either open or selective. During open coding, every possible indicator was identified and categorized to generate as many codes as possible with the overall goal of determining the core variable. The core variable accounts for the majority of the variation of the data. One guideline for open coding is that the researcher should look at what the data is a study of, what category each bit of data falls into, and what is happening in the data. Another guideline is that the researcher must look at the transcript line-by-line (Bailey, 2010).

After the core variable of confidence-building measures was identified, the data was looked at again using selective coding, this time to understand how each piece of data relates to the core variable. Next, this study used theoretical coding to determine the causes, contexts, contingencies, consequences, co-variance, and conditions that emerged from the data. Specifically, bracketing was conducted during coding by (a) locating key phases that speak directly to the phenomena, (b) interpreting the meanings of these phrases, (c) analyzing these recurring features of the phenomenon, (d) re-defining the phenomenon, (e) portraying each theme, and (d) developing a structural synthesis. Throughout the analysis, the researcher used memoing to help connect disparate data and concepts into a comprehensive theory (Bailey, 2010).

When the theory began to take shape and no new information presented itself, the researcher then integrated insights gained from the literature review into the theoretical model developed during the research. Data was not fit into a preconceived hypothesis; instead, the goal was to have the data emerge from constant comparison and analysis. Again, a holistic inductive approach was taken and inclusivity was used to capture the facets of the topic. Next, through sorting, the researcher began to compare memos, integrating and organizing them into a theoretical outline, focused on developing categorical properties and how they influenced the core variable. Once completed, the theoretical outline visually depicted the major concepts, properties, and ideas, and the connections between each of these components. In the final stage, the researcher described in detail the findings, the data that supported the findings, and the logical connections that emerged from the research (Bailey, 2010).

NVivio 10 qualitative data analysis software was used to accomplish data analysis. First, all interviews that met the screening criteria were uploaded into the software tool. Second, a text search query was used to identify the occurrences of the words "trust" and "confidence." Then, each occurrence of the term was reviewed in context to identify and code types of confidence-building measures applied in each situation. A word frequency query was used to determine the words that commonly coincided with "trust" and "confidence." As confidence-building measures were identified, they were grouped into classification areas, and any other related variables that emerged were identified. The researcher recorded memos on possible relationships in the data inside the software tool. Finally, a visualization graph was created showing the types of confidence-building measures employed and the other variables that affect the phenomenon. All data were stored within the NVivo program for verification later, if required.

Once the theoretical model was constructed, the researcher refined the model through triangulation with the data collected during the literature review. The literature review was uploaded into the NVivo program, and the software was used to code and triangulate the literature review findings with the theoretical model. This was accomplished through looking at the major conclusions of the literature and where the literature validated the logic of the theoretical model. Areas of disagreement between the literature and the theoretical model were also examined.

This ensured that the study builds upon what scholars currently know in the field and that the theoretical model was synthesized using the existing body of knowledge. The theoretical model was refined to ensure it included all of the major types of confidence-building measures applicable in the context. Finally, the researcher created a diagram that depicts the central phenomena of confidence-building measure employment and all other identified variables and their relationship to the central phenomena. The researcher's goal was to make the final theoretical model easy to understand and communicate to others.

Lastly, the researcher triangulated the findings with experts identified from the research sample in the method discussed in the data collection section. To triangulate the results, in-depth interviews were conducted with the subject matter experts using the proposed model as a guide. The interviews were uploaded into the NVivo program for analysis. Each interview was analyzed for trends that indicated that the theoretical model should be modified based on the input of the experts. Lastly, the researcher made the final adjustments to the theoretical model and described the findings in further detail in the subsequent sections of the dissertation.

CHAPTER IV: RESULTS

This chapter reports a summary of the results collected using the methodology as described in the previous chapter. The next chapter will discuss and interpret the findings and put the results in the proper academic context. This section will present a summary of the results aligned with the research questions. The results sections will discuss (a) the sample, (b) data collection, (c) data analysis and results.

The question that this research sought to answer was, "How do U.S. service members employ confidence-building measures to build trust over time with key indigenous stakeholders in the contemporary joint operational environment?" The researcher used the following sub-questions:

1. What do the data indicate are the key qualitative statements that provide insight into how U.S. service members use confidence-building measures to build trust with key indigenous stakeholders in the contemporary joint operational environment?

2. What do the data indicate as the major categorical themes of how U.S. service members use confidence building measures to build trust with key indigenous stakeholders in the contemporary joint operational environment?

3. What do the data indicate is the relationship between these major themes of how U.S. service members apply confidence-building measures to build trust with key indigenous stakeholders in the contemporary joint operational environment?

The grounded theory methodology calls for an open approach to the data, not the confirmation of strictly defined variables. Therefore, the research approached the data in an exploratory manner to describe the phenomenon in its fullest and richest context.

Sample

For the creation of the theoretical model, the researcher reviewed existing interviews from the Operational Leadership Experiences (OLE) database ($N = 2,515$). Those that fit the contextual screening criteria as described in the methodology chapter were the sample for creation of the initial theoretical model ($N = 67$). Table 2 depicts the demographics of the

initial sample. Of note, members of the original sample were all male, primarily from the

United States Army, on active duty, held the rank of major, and had only one deployment.

Table 2

Initial Sample Demographics

Characteristic	OLE Database Interviews ($N = 67$)	
	N	Percentage
Gender		
Male	67	100.00%
Female	0	0.00%
Service Nationality		
Australian	1	1.49%
United Kingdom	1	1.49%
United States	65	97.01%
Branch of Military		
Army	65	97.01%
Navy	0	0.00%
Air Force	2	2.99%
Marines	0	0.00%
Duty Status		
Active duty	58	86.57%
Reservist	9	13.43%
Rank		
Sergeant Major	1	1.49%
First Lieutenant	1	1.49%
Major	60	89.55%
Lieutenant Colonel	5	7.46%
Number of Deployments		
1	40	59.70%
2	22	32.84%
3	5	7.46%

This initial sample was screened against set criteria to determine the subject matter experts ($N = 27$). To contact the subjects for further in-depth study, the researcher searched email databases and recorded information for those with valid contact information ($N = 25$). Every member of this potential subject matter expert sample was sent an email message to schedule that in-depth interview. Ten potential subject matter experts contacted the researcher and volunteered for a follow-up interview ($N = 10$). The mean age of the subject matter experts was 39.1, and all of the participants were male, served in the U.S. Army, and were officers at the rank of major. Deployments ranged from two to four (see Table 3).

Table 3

Subject Mater Expert Sample Demographics

Characteristic	Expert Interviews ($N =10$)	
	N	Percentage
Sex		
Male	10	100.00%
Female	0	0.00%
Service Nationality		
United States	10	100.00%
Branch of Military		
Army	10	100.00%
Duty Status		
Active duty	9	80.00%
Reservist	1	20.00%
Rank		
Major	10	100.00%
Deployments		
2	3	30.00%
3	5	50.00%
4	2	20.00%
Specialty Field		
Artillery	1	10.00%
Infantry	3	30.00%
Logistics	3	30.00%
Chemical	1	10.00%
Air Defense	1	10.00%
Civil Affairs	1	10.00%

Data Collection

The theoretical model creation phase of data collection included the use of preexisting online databases of service member interviews. The researcher navigated to the website where the Operational Leadership Experiences database stores information in a searchable format. The interviews were searched using the database search engine to identify interviews that had the occurrence of the required search terms within the transcript, and transcripts of these interviews were subsequently downloaded to the researcher's computer. Once the researcher had retrieved the digital copies and saved them, they were uploaded into the NVivo data analysis program simultaneously. The researcher then read each interview focusing on the descriptions surrounding the key words "trust" or "confidence" to determine contextual relevance.

Functions within the NVivo program were used to code data by highlighting and saving the text as a "node." As themes emerged during coding, the nodes were organized as categories underneath thematic nodes. The nodes and themes were then revised, and numerous data queries were conducted to gain insights into the data and to create the initial theoretical model within the NVivo program.

During the literature triangulation phase of data collection, the researcher uploaded the existing text of the literature review as a separate file in the NVivo program. Then, the literature review was analyzed using the NVivo program to code the text of document and to discern any themes that either supported or refuted the major themes of the theoretical model created in the first phase of data analysis. Various queries were run on the data using the NVivo program to discern insights into the data and draw relevant conclusions. The researcher then exported the relevant data in Excel format to create tables that depicted the key conclusions.

As the research progressed, the researcher contacted the subject matter experts with individual emails, asking them to agree to volunteer for a follow-up interview and to return the signed informed consent form. Each willing subject was contacted to schedule an interview after he had returned the signed consent form. The interviews were conducted and recorded with a digital sound recorder. The framework questions were followed to ensure that each interview contained the critical topics under investigation. The researcher then uploaded the digital files of each subject matter expert interview into the NVivo program for analysis and coding. The data provided by the subject matter experts were coded and the theoretical model was refined accordingly, including characteristics of the theoretical model recommended by the subject matter experts.

Data Analysis and Results

Analysis of Existing Interviews and Theoretical Model Creation

As the grounded theory methodology requires, the researcher coded the data using an open coding methodology to generate as many codes as possible by analyzing each transcript.The core variables of trust were investigated to identify all causes, contexts, contingencies, consequences, co-variance, and conditions that the data indicated. The researcher conducted bracketing to (a) locate the key phases that speak directly to the phenomena, (b) interpret the meanings of these phrases, (c) analyze these recurring features, (d) redefine the phenomenon, (e) portray each theme, and finally, (d) develop a structural synthesis.

Within the existing interviews, the researcher identified 50 different codes that the data indicate relate to building trust. Table 4 depicts the initial open coding results and the number of items coded to each node. Three nodes were coded with over 20 references, six with 10 to 20 references, and 41 with one to nine references.

Table 4

Open Coding Initial results

Node	Coded Items	Node	Coded Items
Partnered activities	29	Listening	4
Cultural differences	23	Overcoming a challenge	3
Time	21	Assisting schools	3
Meeting basic needs	17	Follow up discussions	3
Use of interpreters	14	Incremental success	2
Host nation led activities	12	Understanding personalities	2
Sharing food or drink	10	Medical assistance	2
Building rapport	10	Development projects	2
Collocation with stakeholders	10	Handling requests	2
Positive social interactions	9	Previous experiences	1
Native language use	8	Dealing with corruption	1
Initial distrust	7	Earning respect	1
Unobtrusive security posture	7	Reinforcing institutions	1
Economic assistance	7	Peer-to-peer interaction	1
Regular meetings	7	Making amends	1
Intelligence sharing	7	Displaying patience	1
Conditional trust	6	Training together	1
Partnered operations	6	Food or water assistance	1
Accepting risk	6	Improving local markets	1
Showing / earning respect	5	Agricultural assistance	1
Problem solving	5	Creating jobs	1
Assist vulnerable populations	5	Understanding politics	1
Facilitating communication	5	Negotiated agreements	1
Asking questions	5	Holding conferences	1
Playing sports	4	Building camaraderie	1

As the researcher progressed through bracketing with the existing interviews, connections between the accounts and recognizable themes emerged. The first major theme that emerged from the open coding and analysis was the component of time. In one of the interviews, Major Richard F. stated, "One of the best ways to learn who to trust is through habitual relationships and working with people. Over time, you learn who you can trust and who you can't" (CSI, 2009, p. 9). The data indicates a strong connection between time and trust. In another interview, Major Andrew B. stated:

> *You have to live as close as you can to it and spend as much time as you can with them [indigenous stakeholders]. It's also a trust thing; it builds the trust. They feel you're not just reporting on them but they see you're trying to help them; you're with them and part of the team. That does make a difference. I think it speeds up the relationship you can have with them. Just contact time; you have to live with them and work with them. (CSI, 2011, p. 13)*

The data also indicate that there is a connection between contact time and the success of communication. Major Jason B. stated:

> *When I started working with them towards the end of my deployment they [the indigenous stakeholders] didn't want to talk to me at first and they didn't want to hear anything I had to say. I just kept at it. They didn't like my interpreter at first but we didn't take offense. We just kept on visiting them and showing up everyday talking to them. Eventually we won them over and just earned their trust. (CSI, 2010, p. 9)*

From the existing database of interviews, the researcher then identified that the data indicated communication as another major theme. For example, Major Jason B. stated, "I had this sergeant (E5) talking with the brigade or battalion commander; he would just talk with him and they would listen. He had such credibility because he would just talk with them" (CSI, 2009, p. 9). One sub-theme that the data indicate was the importance of interpreters to building a relationship of trust. In his interview, Major Taly V. stated:

> *If you get in touch with that person you're trying to provide advice to or influence -- that's one of the biggest things you can do to have a successful mission, as well as*

67

having a good reliable interpreter. Build that relationship with your counterparts (and interpreters) because if they don't trust you or trust your judgment it will be that much harder to try and accomplish your mission there. (CSI, 2010, p. 11)

In addition to just interpreters, the data indicated that soldiers who were able to speak a few words of the indigenous language had better success trust building. The interview with Major Robert R. reinforced this point:

Interviewer: What parts of your pre-deployment training, aside from the situational awareness, were most beneficial for you once you got into country?

Major Robert R.: The language. To gain their respect right off the bat was the main thing we needed to do because they [the indigenous stakeholders] don't trust you from anything; they don't know you. As soon as you can gain their respect they'll do anything for you. To be able to go in there and [speak] just the key phrases like, "Hello. How are you? How is your day?" Things like that were huge. (CSI, 2011, p. 5)

The data also indicated that in the communication umbrella, sharing intelligence with the local population was a critical factor in building trust between military and civilian forces. In one case, Lieutenant Colonel Scott F. stated:

Even if they miss, if they [the Iraqi military] hit the right house and the guy's not there, it says we're after you and we're on the case. Then the innocent people are not punished. The innocent people are now more confident in their government, more amenable towards the government, and that causes more cooperation. So maybe an older person will walk over and say, "He's not here right now but I'll keep an eye out for him." Or, "What's your phone number? I'll call you." These are almost confidence-building measures and that's something I learned from Brigadier Hassan. (CSI, 2008, p. 14)

Within the existing interviews, the next major theme that the data indicated was the importance of physical activities to building trust. The data indicated that by simply being collocated with indigenous stakeholders helps build trust. In one example, Major Christian A. stated, "We were able to earn their trust because of the firefight we were in and we fought next to them [the indigenous stakeholders]. Just the fact that we fought next to them immediately earned us their trust" (CSI, 2010, p. 4). Other interviews indicated the

importance of risk and burden sharing. For example, Major Andrell H. said:

> *Often I would travel with my Iraqi counterpart -- COL Khalid and those guys -- with a soft cap and a pistol; no body armor at all. That's what gained respect and wasta [Iraqi slang for personal power] because they knew you trusted them*" (CSI, 2010, p. 23).

The data also indicated that in the physical realm, actions taken directly by host-

nation stakeholders, supported by U.S. service members, helped build confidence during

difficult situations. Major Jasen B.'s description of a joint Iraqi and U.S. mission following a

major explosion provided one example:

> Jasen B.*: It [the vehicle borne explosive device] killed a lot of people and they [the indigenous stakeholders] were concerned about retaliatory death squads coming out. We went out and did a bunch of what they call a show of force or a show of presence. The Army commander was out on the ground talking to the people and we did a couple of shows of presence to show the friendlies that we were there and that we were trying to protect them and also the folks who might not be so friendly; to let them know we were there too.*

> Interviewer: *To try and deter?*

> Jasen B.: *Yeah, a deterrence but also to build the confidence of the people.* (CSI, 2010, p. 8)

The data also indicated that physical activities, such as development projects and

helping disadvantaged populations, led to trust. In one case, Major Eric M. stated:

> *When we weren't going in to do a raid or kill and capture some bad guys in Al-Qaeda it was all about improving relationships with the community. Man, there are definitely some very good, hardworking Iraqis out there who I have some respect for; some guys who have done good things for their communities, their families, and themselves. It was everything from trying to get pump stations along the Tigris working and working with Iraqi engineers or with schoolteachers to try and get the kids back into school. (*CSI, 2010, p. 8)

In analysis of the existing interviews, the data also indicated that physical activities such as participating in sports together could lead to building trust and improve the relationship as well. For example, Major Jason M. stated:

For me it was very enjoyable; I played soccer quite a bit on their helipad. I was pretty much the only American that had played soccer with them and it was done on a cement helipad so it wasn't very good for your knees and ankles. It let them see that we were just like them; that we wanted to do the same things they wanted to do. I wanted to let people who think other thoughts about the U.S. in general see that we were on the same page as them. It paid dividends when you try to actually go talk to them about doing things and convince them that they need to approach new avenues on how to do things. I think it helped a lot. (CSI, 2010, p. 5-6)

The next major theme that the data indicated was critical to building trust was measures that improved relationships. For example, Major Taly V. stated:

Personal relationships. That's probably the key to everything...
...Our reception in the Aburisha brigade turn out to be a good one, mainly, if I should say was due to us taking the time to build a relationship with them and not dictate how things were going to be. Once we gained their trust, they're willing to do anything for us. I think that was what made ours and their success a great one. (CSI, 2010, p. 11)

In some cases, the data indicated that the relationships become very strong. In one interview, Major David W. stated:

We treated them like equals and built mutual friendships. Lieutenant Colonel Sa'lah had been fighting since 1982. I'm a major in the U.S. Army and this is my first combat deployment. He has a lot of experience. It may not be the way I would do it, but it may be the right way for the situation. Once we got to that common ground it worked out really well. (CSI, 2010, p. 8)

Again, sharing risk emerged as a sub-component or relationship as the data indicated that going through a major traumatic event could bring parties closer together. One exemplar of this is what Major Wade G. stated:

It all goes back to relationships and establishing that trust and rapport. That doesn't come immediately. You build it over time. It typically comes at a culminating point usually when something goes wrong and you're there with them. It's just like anything back here. It's cohesive. Going through a challenging event will bring you closer together and when that happens it helps expedite that process of bringing you closer together. (CSI, 2011, p. 10)

The final thematic category that the data indicated was important in building trust were the contextual factors that surround the phenomenon. This theme is important because it highlights many of the limiting factors of confidence-building measure employment. Major Paul M. described one colleague who never was able to trust the Iraqis because of that person's previous experiences. He stated:

> *Our warrant officer was a young private in Desert Storm so he hated going out there. He still didn't trust them [the Iraqis]. We kind of had to drag him. We said, "You have to come out with us. These guys are talking about maintenance." He was in the 82nd so there was some stuff he told us he did and we were like, "Wow!" That's stuff you can't repeat. He didn't trust those guys.*
>
> Interviewer: *Did he ever come around?*
>
> Major Paul M.: *He went out there but he never really enjoyed it because of the experience he had with those guys before.* (CSI, 2009, p. 13)

Likewise, the data indicated that preexisting perceptions and cultural factors held by stakeholders from the host nation play a factor. For example, Major Leslie P. stated:

> *Once you realize that they have the same wants, needs, and desires that we do you'll establish the trust and confidence of the local population. You will be successful. You'll not always be successful; sometimes there are some external factors that may prohibit that when you get into some of the more extremist ideologies but that is the exception.* (CSI, 2009, p. 9)

Another factor that fell into this category of contextual factors was that of corruption. An Interview with Major Andrew B. discussed culture and corruption as an obstacle:

> I wasn't dodging bullets which was good but there was the culture and breaking through some barriers. What we found at the academy was that a lot of the older and senior military were very set in their ways and corruption existed. (CSI, 2010, p. 13)

Table 5 depicts how each node and major theme were categorized into major thematic areas that emerged from the bracketing process: (a) communication, (b) context, (c) physical,

(d) relationship, and (e) time. Of note, the themes were in many cases overlapping and

mutually influencing, and are not rigid categories.

Table 5

Codes Classified by Major Theme

Node	Theme	Node	Theme
Use of interpreters	Communication	Vulnerable populations	Physical
Native language	Communication	Participating in sports	Physical
Regular meetings	Communication	Overcoming a challenge	Physical
Intelligence sharing	Communication	Assisting schools	Physical
Facilitating	Communication	Medical assistance	Physical
Asking questions	Communication	Development projects	Physical
Listening	Communication	Training together	Physical
Follow up discussions	Communication	Food or water assistance	Physical
Handling requests	Communication	Improving local markets	Physical
Negotiated agreements	Communication	Agricultural assistance	Physical
Holding conferences	Communication	Creating jobs	Physical
Cultural differences	Context	Sharing food or drink	Relationship
Initial distrust	Context	Building rapport	Relationship
Conditional trust	Context	Positive social interactions	Relationship
Previous experiences	Context	Showing and earning respect	Relationship
Dealing with corruption	Context	Problem solving	Relationship
Understanding politics	Context	Understanding personalities	Relationship
Partnered activities	Physical	Earning respect	Relationship
Meeting basic needs	Physical	Reinforcing institutions	Relationship
Host nation led activities	Physical	Peer-to-peer interaction	Relationship
Collocation	Physical	Making amends	Relationship
Security posture	Physical	Displaying patience	Relationship
Economic assistance	Physical	Building camaraderie	Relationship
Partnered operations	Physical	Time	Relationship
Accepting risk	Physical	Incremental success	Time

Next, within the existing interviews, the researcher identified the total number of coded items that fell within each major theme and ordered the items by frequency. Table 6 depicts the themes in order from the most frequent to the least frequent. The researcher identified that physical measures occurred most often and time occurred least often in the in the data.

Table 6

Major Themes Ordered by Frequency

Major Theme	Number of Coded Items
Physical	94
Communication	59
Relationship	46
Contextual factors	38
Time	21

Next, a coding query was run using the NVivo program to determine the connections of major themes within the data. Table 7 depicts the number of codes that corresponded with other major themes within the same source. The data indicated the strongest connection between physical and contextual factors themes and between the communication and relationship themes. The data also suggested the weakest connection between the themes of time and both communication and relationship.

Table 7

Major Theme Connections

Major Theme	Physical	Communication	Relationship	Context	Time
Physical	-	7	8	14	8
Communication	7	-	13	6	3
Relationship	8	13	-	5	3
Contextual factors	14	6	5	-	7
Time	8	3	3	7	-

The initial theoretical model was then constructed using the NVivo software. Figure 4 depicts the initial theoretical model derived solely from the OLE interviews. The researcher grouped each of the themes that involved confidence-building measures. The resulting theoretical model depicts the three major variables that time, confidence-building measures, and contextual factors. The term "parent" in the diagram indicates the relationship between categories and subcategories of coded nodes and how the researcher organized the structure of the theoretical model.

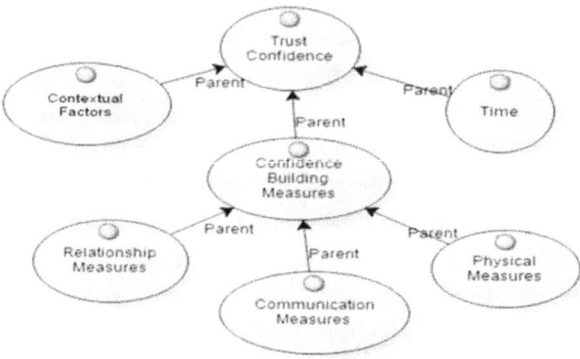

Figure 4. Initial theoretical model.

Literature Review Triangulation

The information in the literature review was examined to determine if the data supported or refuted the major themes identified during the theoretical model creation phase. Table 8 depicts the results of this analysis. The literature indicated that the initial theoretical model is valid, with the strongest connection to the use of communication and physical confidence-building measures.

Table 8

Major Theme Triangulation with Literature Review

Theme	Literature references that support theme	Literature references that refute theme
Physical	17	0
Communication	28	0
Relationship	9	0
Contextual factors	4	0
Time	6	0

Next, a visual depiction of the theoretical model was constructed with the intent of portraying the theoretical model in a comprehensive and easy to understand way. The purpose of this theoretical model depiction was to create a diagram to show to the subject

75

matter experts to obtain their perspective, and subsequently to adjust the model. The

theoretical model depicts the three primary variables and their relationship to the central

phenomena. To make the theoretical model more visually appealing and easy to understand,

the researcher added public use photos of service members engaged in activities related to the

activities the theoretical model describes (DOD Imagery, 2013).

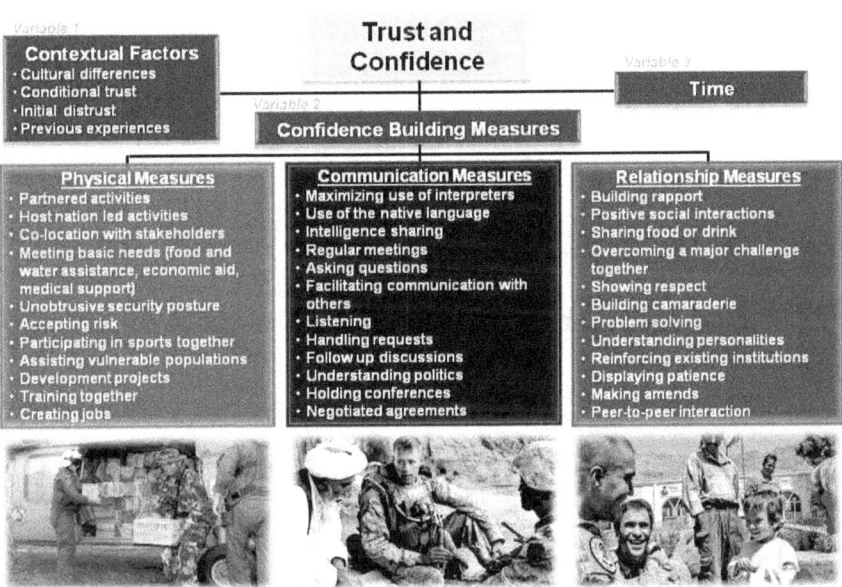

Figure 5. Theoretical model for expert triangulation

Subject Matter Expert Triangulation

Next, the researcher conducted triangulation of the data with a sample of subject matter experts to validate the findings up to this point. The interview questions focused on the nature of confidence-building measures in the context of the contemporary environment. Eight of the 10 interviews were conducted over the phone, one using Skype, and one using Facetime. The researcher made audio recordings of all of the interviews and uploaded them into NVivo for analysis. Even though a list of questions served as a framework, the interviews were conducted in an open format where the subjects could contribute as much or as little as they desired. If appropriate, the researcher used follow-on questions.

Following basic demographic questions, the researcher asked the subjects to detail the specific context in which the military asked them to build trust. This was necessary to provide verification that the expert's experience was relevant and to enable the researcher to understand the contextual nature of the experience. Two of the subjects described building trust with host nation soldiers, one had worked with only civilians, and seven had worked with both civilians and host nation military service members. The data indicated that, in general, the subject matter experts had ample experience with a wide range of indigenous stakeholders. Overall, the subjects described a wide range of contexts and reasons for the felt necessity to build trust. The data indicated that the service members interviewed generally tied the need for building confidence with their overall mission success.

The second framework question focused on whether the experts felt that they were successful in building trust. The purpose of this question was to gauge their overall perception of the results of their confidence-building efforts. Most of the respondents felt that they were successful in building trust ($N = 9$). Only one of the subjects reported his success as mixed.

The third framework question for the subject matter experts focused on how long it took the subjects to build trust. The purpose of this question was to ascertain how long it takes for confidence-building measures to work, the critical temporal aspect. The answers indicated that the time required to build trust took from one month to five months. The one respondent who reported the time to build trust as one month said that he attributed this to the fact that the host nation military and the U.S. service members experienced a high tempo of enemy contact during that period. The majority of respondents reported that it took two ($N = 3$) to three ($N = 4$) months to build trust. One respondent reported that he felt it took anywhere between three and five months to build trust in his situation. One respondent reported that it took from several weeks to seven months to build trust. Therefore, generally the time range that the subjects took to build trust spanned from a few weeks up to seven months.

The fourth question focused on the most important measures the subjects used to build trust. Here, the researcher asked numerous follow on questions to encourage the subjects to provide a richer understanding of what measures they personally used. The data was coded using the NVivo program (see Table 9).

Table 9

Deliberate Confidence-building Measures Used

Measure	Number of Coded Items
Sharing food or drink	4
Open communication	3
Partnered operations	3
Going through enemy contact	2
Physical exercise	2
Allowing them to demonstrate expertise	1
Enabling local governance	1
Getting to know them personally	1
Keeping promises	1
Listening to grievances	1
Living with them	1
Mirroring their security posture	1
Providing answers	1
Recognition awards	1
Shopping at local markets	1
Continual engagements	1
Social events	1
Seeking understanding of local conditions	1
Creating conditions for sustainable jobs	1

The results of the interviews with the subject matter experts indicated that sharing food or drink was the most common measure associated with building trust, followed by open communication, partnered operations, and going through enemy contact together. The researcher identified many previously unidentified measures including (a) listening to grievances, (b) allowing indigenous stakeholders to demonstrate expertise, (c) enabling local governance, (d) getting to know indigenous stakeholders personally, (e) mirroring the security posture of stakeholders, (f) providing recognition awards to indigenous stakeholders, (g) shopping at local markets, and (h) keeping promises made to indigenous stakeholders.

The fifth question focused on understanding the process that the subject applied to build trust, if they applied one at all. This question was critical to determine if experts applied certain measures in a set sequential fashion or if the subject approached the need to build trust in an open and non-structured way. Here, the subjects were in disagreement. Some felt that there was a process ($N = 3$) but the majority felt that it was highly context dependant and there was no established process at all ($N = 7$). Of those who felt there was a process, each reported vastly different processes. Therefore, the data indicated that there is no one universal process for building trust in the context of the contemporary operating environment.

The next question the researcher asked was what advice the subject would give to a future soldier whom the military placed in a similar situation. The purpose of this question was to place the interviewee in a different role and to have him give advice to an imaginary future person in hopes that the indirect nature of the question would illicit new insights. By making the subject of the question an unspecified future soldier, the researcher desired to solicit any negative experiences the subjects may have had but allow them to address their personal shortcoming indirectly instead of confronting them on what they personally did wrong. The results indicated that the subjects would give advice in a variety of key areas as a series of do's and don'ts for potential application in the future (see Table 10).

Table 10

Suggestions for Future Service Members

Suggestion	Number of Coded Items
Understand the culture	4
Act as an intermediary	1
Balance risk	1
Be consistent	1
Choose the correct person to build trust with	1
Choose the correct person to build the trust	1
Conduct a initial 30-day assessment	1
Don't apply a cookie cutter approach	1
Don't assume ignorance	1
Don't assume they share your thoughts	1
Don't disempower them	1
Don't rush them	1
Engage frequently	1
Help provide security	1
Involve them in planning	1
Keep an open mind	1
Never let your guard down	1
Plan to change over time	1
Plan to learn	1
Put them in the lead	1
Relax your security posture (situation dependent)	1
Share food	1
Use actions to communicate	1
Be genuine	1
Use interpreters as cultural advisors	1
Listening	1
Put yourself in their shoes	1

The next question subject matter experts were asked focused on the theoretical model itself. The researcher asked subjects to describe how the theoretical model should be adjusted to have it more adequately depict their experience with building trust. It is important to note that the researcher asked the subject matter experts specifically to detail what the theoretical model was missing based on their own recollection, with the caveat that

other soldiers in different situations may have applied measures that they did not. Generally,

the experts agreed with the theoretical model ($N = 6$; see Table 11).

Table 11

Theoretical Model Comments

Suggestion	Number of Coded Items
Generally concur with theoretical model	6
Add different perceptions of time	2
Agree with context of the situation as important	2
Add balancing of risk	2
Add discovery actions	1
Add establishing open lines of communication	1
Add planning to learn	1
Add problem identification	1
Add problem solving	1
Add shared experience	1
Add the use as interpreters as cultural experts	1
Agree with asking questions measure	1
Agree with holding conferences	1
Agree with physical measures importance	1
Agree with previous experience	1
Agree with sharing intelligence	1
Agree with the importance of time	1
Agree with use of the native language	1

The final question for the experts focused on anything the subject believed the

discussion had not covered. The purpose of this question was to capture any information

related to experiences the subject matter experts may have forgotten to discuss during the

interview or experiences they did not have the opportunity to cover in other portions of the

discussion. This also gave the subjects the freedom to take the discussion any direction that they felt was important over and above what the researcher had considered and ensured data saturation (see Table 12).

Table 12

Open-ended Question

Comment	Number of Coded Items
Must understand cultural norms	2
Admit shortcomings and mistakes	1
Avoid embarrassing anyone in public	1
Designate one person to engage	1
Do not treat them like they are stupid	1
Respect the other party	1
Service members must have high autonomy	1
The personality of the service member is key	1
Information sharing	1
Understand history	1

The researcher included the additional variables that the subjects identified and refined the theoretical model to represent and categorize all of the data holistically. The majority of the respondents concurred with the broad strokes of the theoretical model, and none outright disagreed with it. The researcher decided to retain the generalized representation of the variables and the pictures that visually depict the application of the specific confidence-building measure and to make the needed adjustments as recommended by the subject matter experts.

The researcher adjusted the theoretical model and expanded it into three categories because of the depth of the accounts that the experts described. To cover the phenomenon comprehensively, the initial model was expanded into the following (a) the theoretical model, (b) examples of confidence-building measures, and (c) other lessons learned. The purpose of the theoretical model was to describe and define the variables of confidence-building as indicated by the data and depict how the three variables of context, time, and measures (physical, communication, and relationship) contributed to the phenomena in a generalized way (see Figure 6).

The purpose of the second portion of the theoretical model, the examples, was to describe in detail the measures and to provide useful examples of what service members could do within each category to make the variables operational for practice (see Figure 7). The purpose of the third portion of the theoretical model was to communicate the lessons learned (do's, and don'ts) of confidence-building measures (see Figure 8).

The researcher expected the question that led to these insights to provide data on specific confidence-building measures. Instead, this question provided some very nuanced and deep insights into how service members applied confidence-building measures in this context. The researcher decided to add these to the overall theoretical model so that future service members could benefit from the insights. The resulting three part theoretical model (theory, examples, and lessons learned) comprehensively depicts a visual representation as a summary of the results aligned with the research questions.

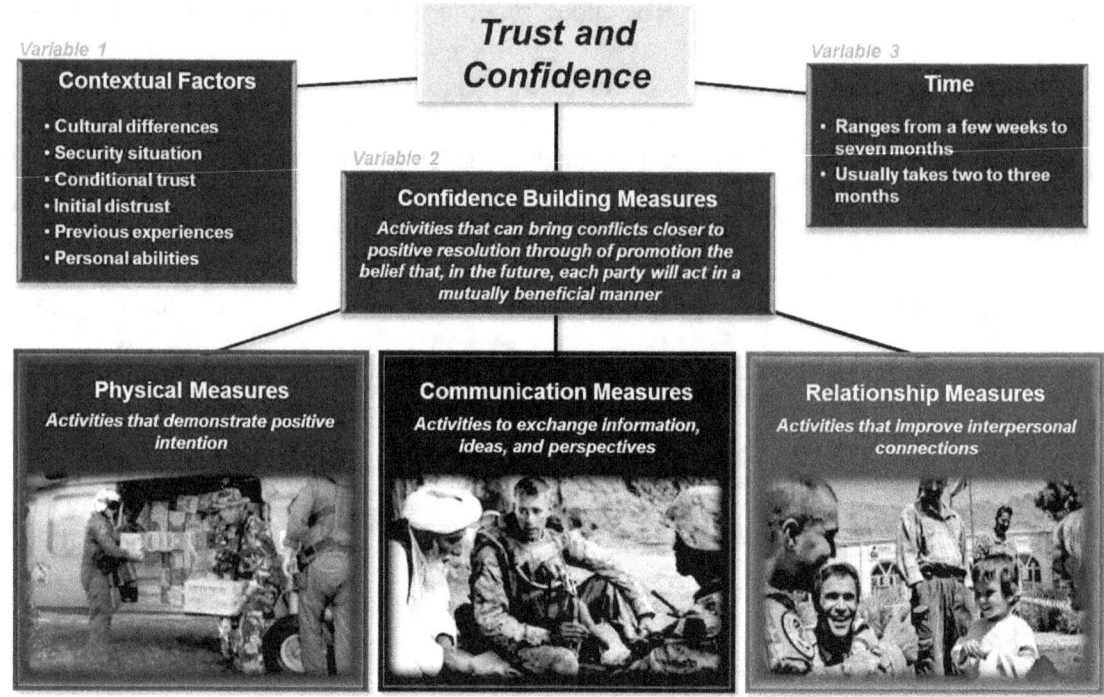

Figure 6. Confidence-building measure use in the contemporary operational environment.

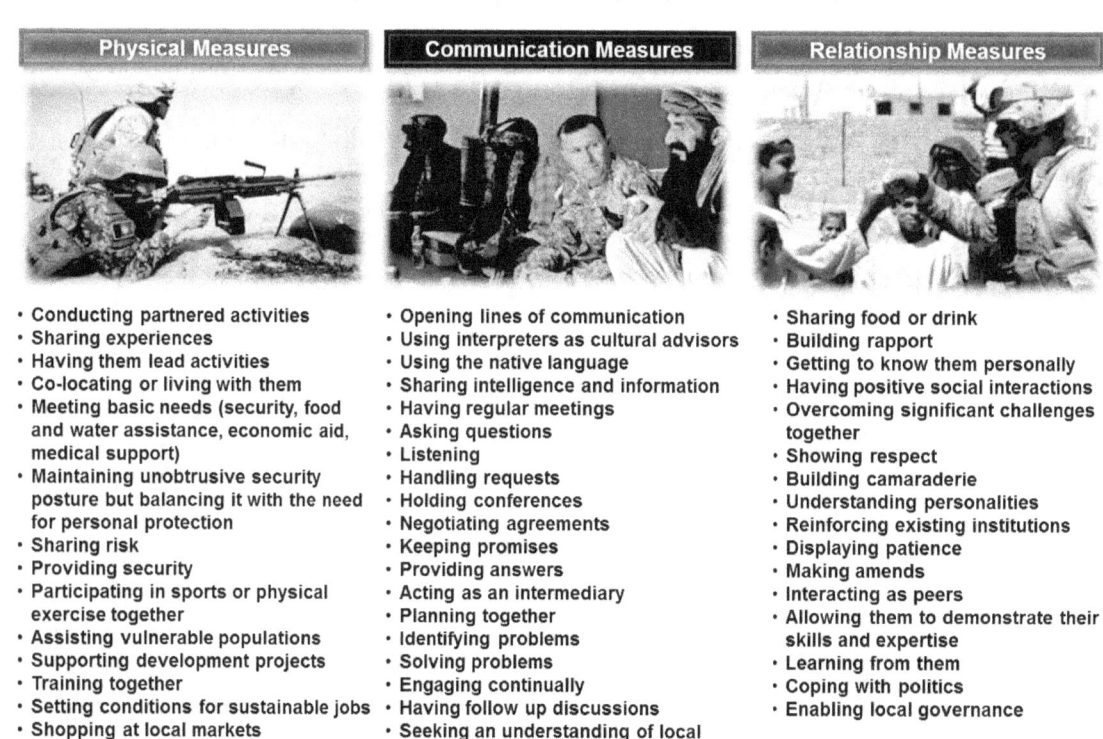

Physical Measures

- Conducting partnered activities
- Sharing experiences
- Having them lead activities
- Co-locating or living with them
- Meeting basic needs (security, food and water assistance, economic aid, medical support)
- Maintaining unobtrusive security posture but balancing it with the need for personal protection
- Sharing risk
- Providing security
- Participating in sports or physical exercise together
- Assisting vulnerable populations
- Supporting development projects
- Training together
- Setting conditions for sustainable jobs
- Shopping at local markets
- Conducting discovery actions

Communication Measures

- Opening lines of communication
- Using interpreters as cultural advisors
- Using the native language
- Sharing intelligence and information
- Having regular meetings
- Asking questions
- Listening
- Handling requests
- Holding conferences
- Negotiating agreements
- Keeping promises
- Providing answers
- Acting as an intermediary
- Planning together
- Identifying problems
- Solving problems
- Engaging continually
- Having follow up discussions
- Seeking an understanding of local conditions

Relationship Measures

- Sharing food or drink
- Building rapport
- Getting to know them personally
- Having positive social interactions
- Overcoming significant challenges together
- Showing respect
- Building camaraderie
- Understanding personalities
- Reinforcing existing institutions
- Displaying patience
- Making amends
- Interacting as peers
- Allowing them to demonstrate their skills and expertise
- Learning from them
- Coping with politics
- Enabling local governance

Figure 7. Examples of confidence-building measures

85

_DO_:
• Keep an open mind and listen
• Plan to change
• Plan to learn
• Choose the correct person to build trust with
• Choose the correct person to build the trust
• Designate one primary point of contact to avoid confusion
• Put them in the lead
• Share food and drink
• Communicate through action
• Give service members a high degree of autonomy
• Conduct a initial 30-day assessment
• Engage frequently
• Admit personal shortcomings and mistakes
• Be genuine
• Put yourself in their shoes

DO NOT:
• Let your guard down
• Embarrass anyone in public
• Treat them like they are stupid
• Apply a cookie cutter approach
• Assume because they do not speak English that they are not intelligent
• Assume they share your thoughts
• Disempower them
• Rush them
• Disrespect them

Figure 8. Confidence-building measures lessons learned.

This chapter discussed the detailed findings of the research and the construction of the final theoretical model. The next chapter will discuss what these findings mean and their potential relevance for academic and operational application and will put the findings in context of other academic research on the subject.

CHAPTER V: DISCUSSION

The purpose of this chapter is to interpret the findings of this study for future research and practice and to discuss the results within the context of other academic research on the subject of confidence-building measures. This chapter will address where the study results converge with or diverge from previous research and will also discuss how the results add to the body of knowledge on the subject. This chapter will also discuss limitations of the study, implications to the field, and suggestions for future research.

The overall need for this study was to address the concern that soldiers need to build confidence with indigenous stakeholders when deployed to dangerous environments presently and in the future. Soldiers will succeed or fail, and possibly live or die, based on their ability to build confidence to reduce and resolve conflict. The purpose of this grounded theory qualitative study was to understand the experiences of military service members who have experienced building trust over time with indigenous populations in Afghanistan and Iraq and to develop a grounded theoretical model of confidence-building measures for use by future service members. The specific problem that this research set out to address was that U.S. service members face a complex problem when building trust with key indigenous stakeholders in the contemporary operating environment and the creation of theory grounded in the data that explains this phenomenon might provide a helpful framework that they can apply to accomplish this difficult task.

The findings in the previous chapter indicate that the synthesis and construction of a comprehensive theoretical model that described the phenomenon of confidence-building in this context is possible. The initial phase of the research, an analysis of achieved interviews, indicated that the variables that led to building trust were (a) contextual factors, (b) time, and

(c) the types of confidence-building measures employed. The data also indicated that the major categories of confidence-building measures employed fell into the categories of (a) physical measures, (b) communication measures, and (c) relationship measures. In addition, the data indicated the strongest connection between physical and contextual factors themes and between communication and relationship themes. The data also suggested the weakest connection between the themes of time and both communication and relationship. The researcher then found that the sources surveyed in the literature review generally supported the initial theoretical model. The researcher then created the theoretical model for subject matter expert verification. The final three-part theoretical model represents a summary of findings for this research.

Interpretation of Findings

Overall, the major findings suggest that when building trust in the joint operational environment, context, time, and confidence-building measures were the thematic variables that affected the phenomena. Additionally, the possible types of confidence-building measures generally fell into the categories of physical, communication, and relationship measures.

The guiding research question which reflected the purpose statement of this research was, "What is a theory, grounded in the data, that explains how U.S. service members apply confidence building measures to build trust with key indigenous stakeholders in the contemporary joint operational environment?" The researcher used the following sub-questions to gain insight and subsequently to construct a grounded theory model:

1. What do the data indicate are the key qualitative statements that provide insight into how U.S. service members use confidence-building measures to build trust with key indigenous stakeholders in the contemporary joint operational environment?

2. What do the data indicate as the major categorical themes of how U.S. service members use confidence-building measures to build trust with key indigenous stakeholders in the contemporary joint operational environment?

3. What do the data indicate is the relationship between these major themes of how U.S. service members apply confidence-building measures to build trust with key indigenous stakeholders in the contemporary joint operational environment?

The findings indicate that the components of confidence-building are (a) contextual factors, (b) the general measures soldiers used to build trust, and (c) time. As the final theoretical model indicates (see Figure 6), three general categories of confidence-building measures emerged, including (a) physical measures, (b) communication measures, and (c) relationship measures.

Contextually, the research indicated that the factors of (a) cultural differences, (b) conditional trust, (c) initial distrust, (d) previous experiences, (e) the security situation, and (f) personal abilities, were important to building trust. Context was an important theme that emerged from this research. Different service members applied different measures with different stakeholders for success. Overall, what may work in one situation may prove the wrong activity in another. What the context variable depicts are all the small factors that, in a complex problem, may affect the phenomena in an unpredictable way. For example, if a service member had previous experiences fighting the population, he or she may never learn to trust members of the population and may always display conditional trust or distrust.

Because the researcher constructed this theoretical model from reported experiences of military service members in Iraq and Afghanistan, one can expect the model to have the highest validity in those contexts. If the military deploys a service member to Africa on a humanitarian assistance mission or within the United States as a response to a natural disaster, one could expect the context of trust to differ substantially. To apply the theoretical model effectively in the future, the findings indicate that a service member must understand the importance of contextual factors and, using sound personal and professional judgment, conduct confidence-building activities as appropriate.

The second theoretical variable that was of the significant importance was time. The research indicates that when soldiers seek to build trust the process took from a few weeks up to seven months, with the average time being two to three months. Time, as a quantitative measure, was a simple variable for this research to identify and categorize. Intuitively, it makes sense that some stakeholders would have different initial levels of trust due to the context variable, and, therefore, it would take service members different amounts of time to achieve trust. For example, if the relationship with a previous U.S. service member was less than optimal, it likely increased the time required for another service member to build confidence and trust. In addition, the research suggests that if the confidence partners faced a significant challenge together, such as an enemy attack, soldiers building trust were able to do so at a more rapid rate. It is also critical to acknowledge that the general perception of time varies between cultures. Because people often do not perceive time in the same way the time required to establish rapport may differ.

The research indicates physical measures, activities that demonstrate positive intention, are the most often employed and the most effective. This makes sense given an environment where a language barrier exists between the parties, observable actions increase in importance. Of these, this research indicates that simply being located together, partnering, and eventually letting the stakeholders from the host nation lead the activities themselves creates huge trust dividends for the soldiers. Many soldiers reported that, in some situations, taking off their body armor, sunglasses, helmets, and even leaving behind their weapons, communicated to the host-nation stakeholders that the U. S. service members were trusting of the stakeholders and that the stakeholder reciprocated trust as a result. One of the unexpected findings of this research was the importance that physical activity and sports has on the trust building process. This ranged from simply doing standard military physical training, to participating in sports, to participating in training events with one another.

In all of the physical measures, the findings indicate the need to find a balance between assuming physical similarity with the stakeholder and the service members' need for personal safety and protection. This is an important contradiction to acknowledge; when building trust, one must assume risk, and to assume risk one may put himself or herself in a situation of vulnerability. In non-permissive environments, opening one's self up to risk could cost the service member his or her life. Not to assume risk could equally increase the risk because the lack of trust that it shows could spur further mistrust. The data indicates that within this equation the service member should strive for a balance, protecting himself or herself, while, at the same time, reaching out to build a relationship with the other party. As this often runs counter to the service member's training and instincts, it is one of the biggest personal challenges to overcome when attempting to build trust with indigenous populations in the joint operational environment.

This research defined communication measures as activities to exchange information, ideas, and perspectives. These measures emerged as the next major category of confidence-building measures that the service members applied. In a situation where parties in conflict speak different languages, the data indicates that communication is critical. For communication itself to succeed, the service member must open the lines of communication, speak as well as listen, and help identify and solve problems using communicative tools.

This all begins with the service member building a thorough understanding of the local environment. Communication measures build the foundation for the relationship measures, the next major category of confidence-building measures.

This research defines relationship measures as activities that improve interpersonal connections. These measures ranged from sharing food or drink, to learning about the other person, to showing patience and understanding. Professionally, the service member should learn from the other party and accept a way of doing things that may be inconsistent with how the service member personally believes things should happen. The service member should share personal details about his life, treat indigenous population members as peers, and, most importantly, admit when he or she has made a mistake. One can characterize relationships between any two humans as a continual give and take and risk and reward; relationships in this context are no different.

The final findings for discussion are the lessons learned for service members in similar situations in the future. Originally, the research included this question in the hopes that subject matter experts who participated in interviews would discuss their own mistakes. They could address personal shortcomings by giving advice to a future soldier in a manner that upholds their own sense of ego while still acknowledging what might not have worked in the field. What the researcher discovered was that the answers to this question were very insightful and informative. These lessons learned presented themselves as a series of heuristic do's and dont's, and, as rules of thumb, provide insights to how future service members should apply the confidence-building theoretical model. The subject matter experts generally describe keeping an open mind, planning to change, and planning to learn. Overall, the advice to the future soldier was to put oneself in the shoes of the other party and not assume that just because the other party does not speak English that they are unintelligent or incapable.

Limitations of Study

Despite the fact that the researcher utilized a grounded theory research methodology, numerous limitations may affect the validity, generalizability, or trustworthiness of the results. As validity is, in general terms, the fit between reality and the findings, the internal and external validity of the findings is a critical topic of discussion to interpret the findings fully. The grounded theory approach uses a small in-depth sample to build a theoretical model; therefore, scholars assume that internal validity, whether the findings fit the subjects' lives and beliefs, is strong. The theoretical model is a reflection of the subjects' lives as recollections and changed throughout the research to reflect the perceptions of the subjects.

Data collection really began with the literature review and establishment of the current baseline of academic knowledge on the subject. Once the researcher established this baseline, he used the 2,515 interviews contained in the Operational Leadership Experiences database to begin to transform the subject from the purely theoretical to the practical. The initial sample of 67 interviews from the existing interviews did not intentionally cover confidence and trust. The Combat Studies Institute conducted those interviews for other purposes, but many interviewees referenced issues of trust-building in the joint operational environment. The researcher analyzed these interviews to construct an initial theoretical model. Then, 10 subject matter experts were asked to reflect upon their experiences and the initial theoretical model, and, out of those dialogues, the researcher was able to identify the phenomena within a larger context. By carefully selecting subject matter experts who had rich, phenomenological experiences and by conducting in-depth follow-on interviews, the researcher was able to gain a full appreciation of the variables involved in building trust. Simply put, by starting with a wide aperture and focusing incrementally on increasingly detailed analyses, one can assume that, in general, the theoretical model represents real perceptions and experiences, and, therefore, one can assume that the findings are internally valid. However, this degree of internal validity is not without limits.

The limitation of this internal validity is associated with the limitation of the study participants themselves--that necessary assumption this research made that the subjects' interviews accurately reflect reality and were not just their rationalization of the experiences. As previously discussed, in research it is generally accepted that people can inject their own personal biases and omit or include information to maintain a positive self-image and to gain acceptance of that image from the external audience, or, in this case, the researcher (Goffman, 1959; Raffel, 2013). Therefore, the specific amount of individual subject bias that entered into this research is truly unknowable and represents one limitation to this research.

The external validity, or how well the findings fit within the external world, is another limitation of this research. If the researcher had the capacity and resources to interview actual host-nation stakeholders with whom the subjects attempted to build trust, then the researcher could have constructed a picture of the phenomenon that had greater external validity. Truly, any researcher, even with unlimited resources, would struggle to formulate this theoretical model in situ. Ideally, the researcher would have access to all parties and would conduct interviews before, during, and after deliberate confidence-building efforts. In a majority of situations, a researcher would find this difficult. In a non-permissive environment, such as Iraq or Afghanistan, this is close to impossible. This obvious gap in external validity was necessary based on the conditions but does give future researchers a valuable area for potential future study.

Another important limitation was the researcher's own past experience and biases. As a soldier, and as a soldier who built trust while deployed to Pakistan, the researcher naturally had preconceived notions of what worked and what did not work in building trust. The grounded theory methodology required that the researcher approach the data in an open and inductive manner. As such, the researcher realized his own gaps in knowledge. Most of these measures were ones that the researcher, because of his own personal biases and preconceived ideas and values, had not previously considered. An example of this was the service members' use of sports, such as soccer, to build confidence. The researcher realized he had much to learn and adopted an attitude of appreciative inquiry characterized the conduct of the research.

The researcher did influence the participants to participate and to cover specific topics of inquiry in a uniform manner. The researcher made every effort not to lead or shape the interviews of the subjects in anyway. Even though the researcher used paraphrasing to clarify statements, at no time did the researcher tell the participants what to say.

Overall, the researcher's perceptions of the phenomena of trust-building expanded significantly. The international relations and political science fields provided the basic structure and conceptual definitions of confidence-building. The literature from the psychology field indicated that the phenomenon of confidence-building was of a much more complex and interpersonal nature. The initial interviews brought the theoretical model to life with practical examples. The subject matter expert interviews helped polish the ideas and deepen the underlying ideas of the theoretical model. From the conceptual underpinnings to the practical measures in the final three-part theoretical model, the research process created

depth, breadth, and context into the scholarly knowledge of the subject that had not existed

before.

Implications for Theory and Research

Within the larger body of literature on the topic, including the conceptual and

theoretical framework of confidence-building, this study fits well. First, it extends the

concept of confidence-building measures into a new, more specified context. By looking at

the micro-level of one-on-one interactions at the individual stakeholder level, this study

added depth to the existing, macro-level view of confidence-building measures between

nation states. This theoretical model represents a grounded theory for use by soldiers using

generalized lessons learned from practical application of the concept. This research found no

study that discussed confidence-building measures in a context that was this specific. The

implication for theory and research are that this research could open interest in other

contexts.

To properly place these findings in the context of the existing literature in the field, it

is important for one to look at the literature by drawing upon sources reviewed in the

literature review and any newer sources published since the proposal was written. First, the

importance of communication confidence-building measures depicted in the model also has

been emphasized by numerous authors in the international relations and political science

fields (Hilali, 2005; Maiese, 2003; Nation, 1989; Osgood, 1959; Raju, 2009; Stimson Center,

2011; Vick, 1988). The model also included physical confidence-building measures which

have been extensively addressed in the literature as well (Borawski, 1986; Burt, 1984;

Higgins, 2001; Hilali, 2005; Maiese, 2003; Nation, 1989; Raju, 2009; Rathmell, 2000;

Stimson Center, 2011; Stockholm Conference, 1986; United Nations, 1975, 1982; UN Center for Disarmament, 1982; Vick, 1988). Relationship measures did come to the forefront in the research findings, which is supported throughout the literature in the political science and international relations fields (Kahn, 2010; Maiese, 2003; Ota, 2009; UN Center for Disarmament, 1982; UN Office for Disarmament, 2009; United Nations, 1982).

There were some major types of confidence-building measures mentioned in the literature that did not play a significant role in the investigated context. One difference between the literature and the model was that the findings did not suggest that economic measures were a major theme as they were in the literature (Higgins, 2001; Kahn, 2010; Raju, 2009; UN Center for Disarmament, 1982). Additionally, the literature indicated that political measures were important (Gottwald et al., 2009; Hilali, 2005; Kahn, 2010; Maiese, 2003; Muniruzzaman, 2010; Raju, 2009; UN Center for Disarmament, 1982; UN Office for Disarmament, 2009; Vick, 1988), and while they were mentioned in the interviews, the data indicated that they did not play a major thematic role. Finally, planning measures did not assume a major thematic role in the model to the same degree as in the literature (Gottwald et al., 2009, Higgins, 2001). Overall, these differences can be attributed to contextual differences between the macro-level interaction of nations and the micro-level interaction between individuals investigated by this research.

In general, the literature from the psychology field reviewed supported the findings as well. When service members built trust, the findings suggest that because the common human need for safety (Maslow, 1954), confidence was built at a faster rate. When service members and their counterparts faced dangerous situations together, their individual need for safety became interlinked with the other party. This mutual interdependence necessitated the formation of a trust bond. Humanistic psychology also mentions encounters where people interact in an open way (Rowan, 2001), and the findings suggest that the more time spent interacting with the other party in this way increased trust.

To ensure that no new literature was published since the research proposal was submitted, the researcher conducted a search of the original databases using the identical search terms that were used during the literature review. One of the sources identified (Wolff, 2013) discussed confidence-building measures in the international relations context in a manner that categorized confidence-building measures in time periods of short, medium, and long term. Even though the context differs from this research study, this is a theoretical idea that is of importance. For this research, if service members employ confidence building in the way suggested by the theoretical model, they will able to act in a way that does not focus on short-term confidence gains without the intent of following through to the mid-range and long-term periods of time. This highlights the criticality of continuity of a relationship. Every year soldiers rotate out, and new soldiers replace them. This necessitates that the service member perform actions to ensure the continuity of trust to the person replacing them. It also raises the uncomfortable question "When the U.S. leaves a nation and all the service members leave, where does this leave the indigenous stakeholders?"

Grabowski (2012), who applied the idea of confidence-building measures to the business world and the financial market, has presented another interesting article that this researcher had not previously identified. He made a fascinating conceptual connection between ethics, reputation, and perception. What is an important point for this research is that confidence-building measures combined with unethical behavior could be expected to prove less effective. In the context of the contemporary operating environment, unethical activities of a few service members, such as the Abu Gahrib prison incident in Iraq, could provoke distrust. This shows the importance of the contextual variable to the overall model. Even if a service member applied the measures as the model suggests, unethical activities of other soldiers could work to establish a context where trust is jeopardized. The implication is that confidence-building measures must be applied ethically and can be negated by factors outside of the service members' immediate control.

Another new article was found that discussed the importance trust. Balliet and Van Lange (2012) presented a meta-analysis of trust-related research and provided a simple, but comprehensive, definition of trust from the perspective of the field of psychology. They have defined trust "as a belief (or expectation) about others' benevolent motives during a social interaction" (p. 2). Also of importance is their research found that when the stakes of the conflict were high, trust became a more important factor in the overall success of conflict resolution. For this research, this means that in the case of service members and those with whom they seek to build trust, because their very lives are at stake, the criticality of trust is paramount. This highlights the importance of this research and the potential impact of the model in the military's contemporary operating environment.

Another interesting article found in the follow-up review was written by Shallcross and Simpson (2012). They conducted an experiment with couples in long-term relationships and put them in different stressful situations to see how they would react. They found that couples with initial higher trust levels were more accommodating, open, and collaborative than those with lower trust levels when facing stress. The importance of the findings for this research are that even if the service members and indigenous stakeholders are not presently going through a conflict, once trust is established, it could provide a beneficial effect when conflicts do arise. This means that service members should not only build trust with those with whom they are in conflict but also with others with whom they wish to keep as supporters.

Another study was found that looked at the cross-cultural implications of trust with preschool children ($N = 144$) from Turkey, China, and England (Lucas, Lewis, Pala, Wong, & Berridge, 2013). The findings indicated that trust varied in many different ways based on the culture background of the children involved. Again, the research in this article was conducted in a very different context from the research conducted in this study. However, it reinforces the importance of understanding the context variable and, more specifically, the cultural perceptions and norms of what constitutes a trusting relationship.

In light of other published research studies, the findings of this study indicate that this theoretical model is an original representation of the phenomenon of confidence-building measures in the joint operational environment. As previously discussed, the grounded theory approach considers all data available, and the researcher used the literature extensively to formulate the initial theoretical model. Therefore, the theoretical model contains insights from the literature, and the literature generally supports the findings. However, there was work that depicts a visual representation of the variables involved in confidence-building in a similar manner. The final theoretical model is an original way to view the use of confidence-building measures in a relevant and potentially valuable way, showing interactions between the various elements of the theoretical model.

The implications of the current study's findings are pertinent to current theory because of the depth of qualitative interviews with the subject matter experts. These soldiers, all of them in life and death situations learned how to adapt to their environments and survive through building mutual trust. If individual soldiers were able to build trust by using elements of this theoretical model, scholars could investigate how other individual actors do the same. The results could have cross-applicability to other contexts where parties could apply this theoretical model to resolve other conflict situations. This theoretical model includes very specific actions that a party can take to garner trust. This takes the idea of confidence-building measures from the broad and conceptual down to the operational and practical level. Simply, it makes confidence-building measures easier to understand and apply.

The implications of the current study's findings for professional practice or applied settings are potentially great as well. Through 2014, the United States will continue to employ service members in Afghanistan. This means that a service member could apply the lessons immediately to the field upon publication of this dissertation. After 2014, this theoretical model will represent one data point of knowledge for how service members addressed the need to build trust. In the future, as the nation deploys soldiers to support national policies and objectives, soldiers could apply the model as well. Additionally, other potential applications exist for organizational consultants or other conflict resolution professionals in other contexts.

Recommendations for Further Research

The findings indicate that scholars and practitioners have much to learn on the application of confidence-building measures in a contemporary context. The literature indicates on the macro-level, in the context nation state interactions, scholars and practitioners understand and apply the idea of confidence-building measures. However, with the rise of violent non-nation state actors on the contemporary world stage, many parties in conflict have become difficult to define using a nation-state framework. Therefore, if confidence-building measures are to find a practical use in the new world order, researchers should pursue other micro-level interactions for investigation.

One potential future research question is "How do other populations apply confidence-building measures in contemporary contexts?" Researchers could gain much deeper insights through looking at different populations and their practices and perceptions. In addition, scholars should investigate the use of confidence-building measures (or lack thereof) in contemporary conflicts by looking at the micro-interactions between parties engaged to resolve contemporary conflicts.

Ideally, as a complement and counterpoint to this research, if scholars investigated the perceptions of Afghanistan and Iraqi stakeholders, they could gain a much deeper understanding of what occurred on both sides, strengthening the theoretical model and academic understanding. Therefore, another future research question is "How did indigenous stakeholders in Iraq and Afghanistan build trust with American stakeholders in the contemporary operational environment?" By answering this research question, the researcher could complete the picture of the confidence-building phenomena from the other party's perspective. Through modifying the theoretical model from this perspective, a more comprehensive and externally valid model would result.

Another potential research question is "How have soldiers built trust with key indigenous stakeholders in past conflicts?" Researchers could look deeper into the history of confidence-building measure application at the micro-level between soldiers and indigenous stakeholders from past conflicts. A large number of interviews of soldiers from World War II, Korea, Vietnam, and the Gulf War exist in database archives. By examining the context of the environment in which the soldier builds confidence, future researchers could increase the validity of the theoretical model.

Within the conflict resolution field, researchers could gain great insights into the population variations in confidence-building measure application between businesses, legal disputants, or marital partners. Another potential research question is "How do conflict resolution professionals apply confidence-building measures in contemporary practice?" Practitioners in the conflict resolution field could apply the theoretical model developed in this research. However, without additional specific research, one could view the validity of the theoretical model in new contexts, such as mediation, as spurious, at best.

In this study, the researcher applied a qualitative approach to formulate and refine a theoretical model of trust-building. Vast opportunities exist to research the phenomena quantitatively. Perhaps one of the most interesting areas of research today is the effort to map the functions of the human brain. If researchers had access to fMRI equipment, subjects could go through trust building scenarios in a laboratory context, and the researchers could observe the bio-psychological trust functions within the brain itself. Additionally, a quantitative survey of service members' perceptions before, during, and immediately after they return from deployment could capture valuable trust lessons, as well as those in other areas of interest.

Conclusion

In the contemporary world, the United States has asked its service members to do much more than simply fight the nation's wars. The use of force in contemporary conflicts is not simple; the enemy is not always easy to identify and is often even more difficult to understand. In conflicts where host nation civilians or military members can turn on a U.S.

service member at any moment, learning how to trust and build trust becomes a critical skill for survival that soldiers may need to possess. The nature of contemporary conflicts and anticipated future conflicts is that soldiers, sailors, airmen, and marines will likely find themselves in similar situations to Iraq and Afghanistan. Their ability to build confidence will remain critical to mission accomplishment and personal survival.

During development, the theory was grounded in the data to describe a phenomenon in one specific context. However, in addition to military applications, this model could provide a way for other conflict resolution professionals to approach building confidence where trust does not exist. The theoretical model provides one lens through which to view a very complex and human phenomena, and rightfully, this study comes with a cautionary disclaimer. What worked in one area, in one situation, for one soldier, may not work in the next. This study provides one data point for how those in conflict can face and overcome the challenges to building trust. It will always depend on the individual service member to apply his or her own personal and professional judgment to the unique situation.

This study represents an in-depth look at the potential menu of options for the future soldier to select from and apply during confidence-building activities. Simply applying these measures in a stepwise manner is not a guaranteed recipe for success. Service members will have to listen, learn, and grow alongside those with whom they hope to build trust. Though understanding context and applying physical, communication, and relationship confidence-building measures over time, service members have a valuable framework to succeed in a difficult mission and return home safe—the overall goal of their unit, their family, and the nation.

References

Alvesson, M., & Sandberg, J. (2011). Generating research questions through problematization. *Academy of Management Review*, *36*(2), 247-271.

American Psychological Association. (2012). *Ethics code updates to the publication manual.* Retrieved from http://www.apa.org/ethics/code/manual-updates.aspx

Angus, C. (2010). *The phenomenological approach.* Retrieved from http://upetd.up.ac.z a/thesis/submitted/etd-01112007-142201/unrestricted/06 chapter6.pdf

Army Research Institute. (2012). *Obtaining approval for a survey of U.S. Army personnel.* Retrieved from http://www.hqda.army.mil/ari/pdf/

Aslin, T., & Rothschild, M. (1987). An introduction to a cognitive-behavioral perspective of consumer behavior. *Advances in Consumer Research*, *14*(1), 566.

Bailey, M. (2010). *Shouldering: A grounded theory of helping relationships.* (Unpublished doctoral dissertation). Fielding Graduate University, Santa Barbara, CA. Retrieved from http://search.proquest.com/docview/757929830?accountid=39364.

Balliet, D., & Van Lange, P. M. (2012). Trust, conflict, and cooperation: A meta-analysis. *Psychological Bulletin EBSCOHost.* Retrieved from http://web.ebscohost.com/ehost /pdfviewer/pdfviewer?sid=7fb72c8c-adce-401a-9ecc-9293f4ba2bf1%40sessionmgr114 &vid=7&hid=120

Banerjee, M. (2010). Addressing nuclear dangers: Confidence-building between India-China-Pakistan. *India Review, 9*(3), 345-363.

Barabasi, A. (2009). Scale-free networks: a decade and beyond. *Science, 325*(5939), 412-413.

Barbour, R. (2001). Checklists for improving rigour in qualitative research: A case of the tail wagging the dog? *British Medical Journal, 322*(7294). Retrieved from http://www.ncbi.nlm.nih.gov/pmc/articles/PMC1120242/

Belasco, A. (2009). *Troop levels in the Afghan and Iraq wars, FY2001-FY2012: Cost and other potential issues.* Retrieved from http://www.fas.org/sgp /crs/nat sec/R40682.pdf

Ben-Dor, G. & Dewitt, D. (Eds.). (1994). *Confidence-building measures in the Middle East*. Boulder: Westview Press.

Bens, I. (2005). *Advanced facilitation strategies: Tools & techniques to master difficult situations*. San Francisco: John Wiley & Sons.

Bhandar, D. (2008). Migration, culture conflict, crime and terrorism. *Journal of International Migration and Integration, 9*(3), 337-342.

Braumoeller, B. (2008). Systemic politics and the origins of great power conflict. *The American Political Science Review, 102*(1), 77-93.

Burns, N. & Grove, S. (2010). *Understanding nursing research.* Retrieved from http://books.google.com/books/about/Understanding_Nursing_Research.html?id=Y9 T3QseoHiYC

Burt, R. (1984). Building confidence: Strategy for enhanced security. *Harvard International Review, 6*(5), 23-29.

Borawski, J. (Ed.) (1986). *Avoiding war in the nuclear age: Confidence-building measures for crisis stability.* Boulder, CO: Praeger.

Bosa, P., Terburga, D. & van Honka, J. (2010). Testosterone decreases trust in socially naïve humans. *Proceedings of the National Academy of Sciences, 10*(22), 9991–9995.

Bowen, N. (2008). Security forces cooperate along Afghanistan-Pakistan border. *American Forces Press Service.* Retrieved from http://www.militaryconnection.com /news/march-2008/border-forces-cooperate.htm

British Association for Behavioural and Cognitive Psychotherapies. (2011). *What is CBT?* Retrieved from http://www.babcp.com/Public/What_is_CBT.aspx

Brown, A. (2007). Perestroika and the end of the Cold War. *Cold War History, 7*(1), 1-17.

Brownlee, J. (2007). *Complex adaptive systems: Technical report 070302.* Centre for Information Technology Research. Retrieved from http://citeseerx.ist.psu.edu /viewdoc/download?doi=10.1.1.70.7345&rep=rep1&type=pdf

Byrne, S. & Senehi, J. (2009). Revisiting the CAR field. In D. Sandole, S. Byrne, I. Sandole-Staroste, & J. Senehi (Eds.) *Handbook of conflict analysis and resolution* (pp. 525-530). New York: Routledge.

Carter, M., Forys, K., & Oswald, J. (2008). The cognitive-behavioral model. In A. Hersen, & M. Gross (Eds.), *Handbook of clinical psychology, volume 1: Adults* (pp. 171-201). Hoboken: John Wiley & Sons.

Center for Army Lessons Learned. (2010). *Newsletter 11-03: Iraq provincial reconstruction team handbook.* Retrieved from http://usacac.army.mil/cac2/call/docs/11-03/index.asp

Chevrier, M. (1998). Biological weapons proliferation: reasons for concern, courses of action. *Stimson Report*. Retrieved from http://www.stimson.org/books-reports/biological-weapons-proliferation-reasons-for-concern-courses-of-action/

Chomsky, N. (1982). *Language and the study of the mind*. Retrieved from http://www.marxists.org/reference/subject/philosophy/works/us/chomsky.htm

Combat Studies Institute (CSI). (2012). *Operational leadership experiences project (OLE)*. Retrieved from http://usacac.army.mil/CAC2/CSI/OLEProject.asp

Combat Studies Institute (CSI). (2008). Interview with LTC Scott F. *Operational leadership experiences project (OLE)*. Retrieved from http://usacac.army.mil/CAC2/CSI/OLEProject.asp

Combat Studies Institute (CSI). (2009). Interview with Major Paul M. *Operational leadership experiences project (OLE)*. Retrieved from http://usacac.army.mil/CAC2/CSI/OLEProject.asp

Combat Studies Institute (CSI). (2009). Interview with Major Richard F. *Operational leadership experiences project (OLE)*. Retrieved from http://usacac.army.mil/CAC2/CSI/OLEProject.asp

Combat Studies Institute (CSI). (2010). Interview with Major Andrell H. *Operational leadership experiences project (OLE)*. Retrieved from http://usacac.army.mil/CAC2/CSI/OLEProject.asp

Combat Studies Institute (CSI). (2010). Interview with Major Christian A. *Operational leadership experiences project (OLE)*. Retrieved from http://usacac.army.mil/CAC2/CSI/OLEProject.asp

Combat Studies Institute (CSI). (2010). Interview with Major David W. *Operational leadership experiences project (OLE)*. Retrieved from http://usacac.army.mil/CAC2/CSI/OLEProject.asp

Combat Studies Institute (CSI). (2010). Interview with Major Eric M. *Operational leadership experiences project (OLE)*. Retrieved from http://usacac.army.mil/CAC2/CSI/OLEProject.asp

Combat Studies Institute (CSI). (2010). Interview with Major Jasen B. *Operational leadership experiences project (OLE)*. Retrieved from http://usacac.army.mil CAC2/CSI/OLEProject.asp

Combat Studies Institute (CSI). (2010). Interview with Major Jason B. *Operational leadership experiences project (OLE)*. Retrieved from http://usacac.army.mil/CAC2/CSI/OLEProject.asp

Combat Studies Institute (CSI). (2010). Interview with Major Jason B. *Operational leadership experiences project (OLE)*. Retrieved from http://usacac.army.mil /CAC2/CSI/OLEProject.asp

Combat Studies Institute (CSI). (2010). Interview with Major Jason M. *Operational leadership experiences project (OLE)*. Retrieved from http://usacac.army.mil /CAC2/CSI/OLEProject.asp

Combat Studies Institute (CSI). (2010). Interview with Major Leslie P. *Operational leadership experiences project (OLE)*. Retrieved from http://usacac.army.mil /CAC2/CSI/OLEProject.asp

Combat Studies Institute (CSI). (2010). Interview with Major Taly V. *Operational leadership experiences project (OLE)*. Retrieved from http://usacac.army.mil /CAC2/CSI/OLEProject.asp

Combat Studies Institute (CSI). (2011). Interview with Major Robert R. *Operational leadership experiences project (OLE)*. Retrieved from http://usacac.army.mil /CAC2/CSI/OLEProject.asp

Combat Studies Institute (CSI). (2011). Interview with Major Andrew B. *Operational leadership experiences project (OLE)*. Retrieved from http://usacac. army.mil /CAC2/CSI/OLEProject.asp

Combat Studies Institute (CSI). (2011). Interview with Major Wade G. *Operational leadership experiences project (OLE)*. Retrieved from http://usacac.army.mil /CAC2/CSI/OLEProject.asp

Costa, A. (2003). Trust. In Spielberger, C. (Ed.), *Encyclopedia of applied psychology.* (pp. 611-620).

Creswell, J. (2004). *Educational research: Planning, conducting, and evaluating quantitative and qualitative research.* New York: Prentice Hall.

Department of Defense. (2008). *Joint publication 3-57: Civil-military operations.* Retrieved from http://www.fas.org/irp/doddir/dod/jp3_57.pdf

Department of Defense. (2012). *Capstone concept for Joint operations.* Retrieved from http://www.jfcom.mil/newslink/storyarchive/2009/CCJO_2009.pdf

Department of Defense. (2010). *Joint operating environment.* Retrieved from www.jfcom.mil/newslink/storyarchive/2010/JOE_2010_o.pdf

Department of Defense. (2011). *Joint publication 3-0: Joint operations.* Retrieved from http://www.dtic.mil/doctrine/new_pubs/jp3_0.pdf

Department of Defense. (2012). *Sustaining U.S. global leadership: Priorities for 21ˢᵗ Century Defense.* Retrieved from http://www.defense.gov/news/Defense_ Strategic_ Guidance.pdf

Department of Defense Imagery. (2013). Frequently Asked Questions (FAQ). Retrieved from http://www.defenseimagery.mil/help/faq.html#using

Dimoka, A. (2010). Brain mapping of psychological processes with psychometric scales: An fMRI method for social neuroscience. *NeuroImage, 54,* S263–S271.

Egan, T. (2002). *Advances in developing human resources.* Retrieved from www.hu.liu.se /larc/...and.../Grounded20theory_3pdf.pdf

Emamjomehzadeh, S., & Jahanshahrad, H. (2003). Regional security regime, confidence and security building measures within the context of Arab-Israeli disputes. *Alternatives: Turkish Journal of International Relations, 2*(3/4), 63-85.

Evans, S., Shergill, S. & Averbeck, B. (2011). Oxytocin decreases aversion to angry faces in an associative learning task. *Neuropsychopharmacology, 35*(13), 2502–2509.

Henwood, K., & Pidgeon, N. (2003). Grounded theory in psychological research. In P. M. Camic, J. E. Rhodes, L. Yardley (Eds.), *Qualitative research in psychology: Expanding perspectives in methodology and design* (pp. 131-155).

Holland, J. (1992). Complex adaptive systems. *Daedalus. 1*(121), 17-30.

Hossain, R. (2012), Afghanistan: Green-on-blue attacks in context. *Understanding War.* Retrieved from http://www.understandingwar.org/green-on-blue/

Fearon, J. (1995). Rationalist explanations for war. *International Organization. 49*(3), 379 – 414.

Fox, S., & Spector, P. (1999). A model of work frustration-aggression. *Journal of Organizational Behavior, 20*(6), 915-931.

Frankfort-Nachmias, C. & Nachmias, D. (2008). *Research methods in the social science*s (7ᵗʰ ed.). New York: Worth.

Friedman, G. (2009). *The next 100 years: A forecast for the 21st century.* New York: Doubleday.

Furlong, G. (2005). *The conflict resolution toolbox: Models & maps for analyzing, diagnosing, and resolving conflict.* Mississauga, Ontario: John Wiley & Sons.

Gigerenzer G. & Selten, R. (2005). *Bounded rationality: The adaptive toolbox.* New York, NY: Cambridge University Press.

Giles, H. (2007). Transforming conflict: Communication and ethnopolitical conflict. *Journal of Communication, 57*(2), 413-414.

Gillian, B., Crawford, A., & Buczek, K. (1987). *Compendium of confidence-building proposals.* Operational Research and Analysis Establishment (ORAE) Extra-mural Paper Number 45.

Gilpin, R. (1981). *War and change in world politics.* New York, NY: Cambridge University Press.

Glaser, B. (2005). Military confidence-building measures. *American Foreign Policy Interests, 27*(2), 91-104.

Glaser, B. (1965). The constant comparative method of qualitative analysis. *Social Problems, 12*(4), 436-445.

Glaser, B. (1978). *Theoretical sensitivity: Advances in the methodology of grounded theory.* Mill Valley, CA: Sociology Press.

Glaser, B. (1992). *Basics of grounded theory analysis.* Mill Valley, CA: Sociology Press.

Glaser, B. (1998). *Doing grounded theory: Issues and discussions.* Mill Valley, CA: Sociology Press.

Glaser, B. (2001). *The grounded theory perspective: Conceptualization contrasted* with *description.* Mill Valley, CA: Sociology Press.

Glaser, B., & Strauss, A. (1967). *The discovery of grounded theory: Strategies for qualitative research.* Mill Valley, CA: Sociology Press.

Goffman, E. (1959). *The presentation of self in everyday life.* New York, NY: Doubleday.

Goodby, J., & Barry, R. (1996). The Stockholm conference on confidence- and security-building measures and disarmament in Europe. *International Negotiation, 1*(2), 187-203.

Gottwald, E., Hasenclever, A., & Kamis, B. (2009). Confidence-building measures, joint democracy and disputes among (former) rivals. *Conference Papers – International Studies Association, 1*(22), 82-91.

Grabowski, K. (2012). Corporate harmony and confidence building spheres on the financial market. *Journal of International Business Ethics, 5*(2), 38-44.

Hilali, A. (2005). Confidence- and security-building measures for India and Pakistan. *Alternatives: Global, Local, Political, 30*(2), 191-222.

Higgins, H. (2001). Applying confidence-building measures in a regional context. *Institute for Science and International Security.* Retrieved from http://www.google.com /url?sa=t& source=web&cd=2&ved=0CB8QFjAB&url=http

Hunt, R. (1995). *Pacification: The American struggle for Vietnam's hearts and minds.* Boulder, CO: Westview.

Jorgen-Holst, J. (1983). Confidence-building measures: A conceptual framework. *Survival, 25*(1), 2-15. Retrieved from http://link.aip.org/link/?PSI/5434/270/1&Agg=doi

Johnstone, I., & Corbin, E. (2008). Introduction - the US role in contemporary peace operations: A double-edged sword?. *International Peacekeeping, 15*(1), 1-17.

The Judge Advocate General's School. (2006). *Service member's guide to the civil service relief act.* Retrieved from https://www.dmdc.osd.mil/appj/scra/scraHome.do

Kahn, F. (2010). Prospects for Indian and Pakistani arms control and confidence building measures. *Naval War College Review, 63*(3), 107-121.

Kelman, H. (2009). A social-psychological approach to conflict analysis and resolution. In D. Sandole, S. Byrne, I. Sandole-Staroste, & J. Senehi (Eds.) *Handbook of conflict analysis and resolution* (pp. 170-183). New York: Routledge.

Kimmage, M. (2010). Atomic historiography. *Reviews in American History, 38*(1), 145-152.

Krepon, M., McCoy, D., & Rudolph, M. (1993). *A Handbook for confidence building measures.* The Stimson Center. Retrieved from http://books.google. com/books /about/A_handbook_of_confidence_building_measur. html?id=_gq5AAAAIAAJ

Krepon, M., Newbill, M., Khoja, K., & Drezin, J. (1999). *Global confidence-building: New tools for troubled regions.* New York, NY: St. Martin's.

Krueger, F., McCabe, K., Moll, J., Kriegeskorte, N., Zahn, R., Strenziok, M., ...& Grafman, J. (2007). Neural correlates of trust. *Proceedings of the National Academy of Sciences, 104*(50), 20084–20089.

Krulak, C. (1999) The strategic corporal: Leadership in the three block war. *Marines Magazine.* Retrieved from http://www.au.af.mil/au/awc/awcgate /usmc/strategic_corporal.htm

Lachowski, Z. (2010). Half-century of arms control: A tentative score sheet. *Polish Quarterly of International Affairs, 19*(4), 40-65.

Landau, D., & Landau, S. (1997). Confidence-building measures in mediation. *Mediation*

Quarterly, 15(2), 97-103.

Lorenz, E. (1962). Deterministic nonperiodic flow. *Journal of Atmospheric Sciences, 20,* 130-141.

Lucas, A. J., Lewis, C., Pala, F., Wong, K., & Berridge, D. (2013). Social-cognitive processes in preschoolers' selective trust: Three cultures compared. *Developmental Psychology, 49*(3), 579-590.

Mahoney, M. (1977). Reflections on the cognitive-learning trend in psychotherapy. *American Psychologist, 32,* 5-13.

Maslow, A. (1943). A theory of human motivation. *Psychological Review,* 50(4), 370-396.

Mason, M. (2010). Sample size and saturation in PhD studies using qualitative interviews. *Forum: Qualitative social research, 11*(3).

Mayring, P. (2011). On generalization in qualitatively oriented research. *Forum: Qualitative Social Research, 8*(3). Retrieved from http://www.qualitative-research.net/index. php/fqs/article/view/291/641

McKavitt, P. (2013). So, you're going to be an advisor? Ten easy to follow recommendations to help you become an effective military advisor. *Small Wars Journal.* Retrieved from http://smallwarsjournal.com/jrnl/art/so-you%E2%80%99re-going-to-be-an-advisor

McQuaid, J., & Carmona, P. (2004). *Peaceful mind.* Oakland, CA: New Harbinger Publications.

Moore, C. (2003). *Negotiation.* Retrieved from http://www.au.af.mil/au/awc/awcgate /army/usace/negotiation.htm

Muniruzzaman, A. (2010). Presentation on confidence-building measures and confidence and security building measures. *Bangladesh Institute of Peace and Security Studies (BIPSS).* Retrieved from http://www.bipss.org.bd/download/CBM.ppt

Milburn, T. (2000). Inventing peacekeeping. *PsycCRITIQUES, 45*(1), 45-48.

Morgenstein, M. & Popalzai, M. (2013). U.S. Green Beret among those killed in Afghan attack. *CNN.* Retrieved from http://www.cnn.com/2013/03/11/world/asia/afghanistan-insider-attack

Nation, J. (1989). *Utility of de-escalatory confidence-building measures.* Retrieved From http://oai.dtic.mil/oai/

National Intelligence Council. (2002). *Mapping the global future.* Retrieved from www.foia.cia.gov/2020/2020.pdf

Nolan, C., & Burleigh, M. (2012). Moral combat: Good and evil in World War II. *Ethics & International Affairs: Academics Stand Against Poverty, 26*(2), 286-288.

Obi, C. (2010). Oil as the "curse" of conflict in Africa: Peering through the smoke and mirrors. *Review of African Political Economy, 37*(126), 483-495.

Olsen, E. (2010). Class conflict and industrial location. *Review of Radical Political Economics, 42*(3), 344-352.

Oracle Thinkquest. (2011). *Timeline of the Cold War.* Retrieved from http://www. thinkquest.org /pls/html/think.site?p_site_id=10826

Organization of American States (OAS). (1997). *Confidence- and security-building measures in the Americas.* Retrieved from http://www.oas.org/juridico/english/ga-res96/Res-1409.htm

Ota, F. (2009). Conflict prevention and confidence-building measures between Japan and China. *International Assessment and Strategy Center.* Retrieved from http://www.strategycenter.net/research/pubID.192/pub_detail.asp

Osgood, C. (1959). Suggestions for winning the real war with communism. *Journal of Conflict Resolution, 3*, 295-325.

Osgood, C. (1962). *An alternative to war or surrender.* Urbana: University of Illinois Press.

Parish, T., & Barness, R. (2009). Personality: is it a product of nature, nurture, and/or personal choice?. *Education, 130*(1), 151-152.

Patton, M. (1990). *Qualitative evaluation and research methods* (2nd ed.). Nwbury Park, CA: Sage.

Pilisuk, M., & Skolnick, P. (1968). Inducing trust: A test of the Osgood proposal. *Journal of Personality and Social Psychology, 8*(21), 121-133.

Powell, R. (1996). Uncertainty, shifting power, and appeasement. *The American Political Science Review, 90*(4), 749-764.

Raffel, S. (2013). The everyday life of the self: Reworking early Goffman. *Journal of Classical Sociology, 13*(1), 163-178.

Rathmell, A. (2000). Building confidence in the Middle East: Exploiting the information. *Journal of Palestine Studies, 29*(2), 5-19.

Raju, A. (2009). Maritime confidence-building measures between India and Pakistan. *Pakistan Journal of International Relations, 1*(1), 14-25.

Rangell, L. (1969). Choice-conflict and the decision-making function of the ego: A psychoanalytic contribution to decision theory. *International Journal of Psycho-Analysis,50*(1), 425-452.

Rennison, C., & Planty, M. (2003). Nonlethal intimate partner violence: Examining race, gender, and income patterns. *Violence and Victims, 18*(4), 433-43.

Rogers, C. (1980). *A way of being.* Boston, MA: Houghton Mifflin

Rousseau, D., Sitkin, S., Burt, R., & Camerer, C. (1998). Not so different after all: A cross-discipline view of trust. *Academy of Management Review, 23*(3), 393-404.

Rowan, J. (2001). *Ordinary ecstasy: The dialectics of humanistic psychology* (3rd ed.). London: Routledge.

Salem, W. & Kaufman, E. (2009). From diagnosis to treatment: Toward new shared principles for Israeli–Palestinian peacebuilding. In D. Sandole, S. Byrne, I. Sandole-Staroste, & J. Senehi (Eds.) *Handbook of conflict analysis and resolution* (pp. 437-445). New York: Routledge.

Sandole, D., Byrne, S., Sandole-Staroste, I. & Senehi, J. (Eds.) (2009). *Handbook of conflict analysis and resolution.* Routledge. New York: Routledge.

Schelling, T. (1984). Confidence in crisis. *International Security, 4*(56), 55-66.

Shallcross, S. L., & Simpson, J. A. (2012). Trust and responsiveness in strain-test situations: A dyadic perspective. *Journal of Personality and Social Psychology, 102*(5), 1031-1044.

Steinberg, G. (2004). From diagnosis to treatment: Toward new shared principles for Israeli–Palestinian peacebuilding. In Schnabel, A. & Carment, D. (Eds.) *Conflict prevention: From rhetoric to reality.* (pp. 258-285). Ottawa: Lexington.

Stimson Center. (2011). *Confidence building measures.* Retrieved from http://www.stimson .org/topics/confidence-building-measures/

Strauss, A. & Corbin, J. (1998). *Basics of qualitative research: Grounded theory procedures and techniques.* Thousand Oaks, CA: Sage.

Simmons, O. (2011). *What is grounded theory?.* Retrieved from http://www.groundedtheory.com/what-is-gt.aspx

Singh, S. (1998). Building security and confidence with China. *Across The Himalayan Gap.* Retrieved from www.ignca.nic.in/ks_41063.htm

Sutton, C. & David, M. (2004). *Social research: The basics.* New York, NY: Sage.

Thomas, D. (2005). Human rights ideas, the demise of communism, and the end of the cold war. *Journal of Cold War Studies, 7*(2), 110-141.

Thomson, S. (2011). Sample size and grounded theory. *Journal of Administration and Governance, 5*(1), 45-52.

Trochim, W. (2006). *External validity.* Retrieved from http://www.socialresearchmethods .net/kb/external.php

United Nations. (1975). *Conference on security and co-operation in Europe final act, 1 August 1975.* Retrieved From http://www.hri.org/docs/Helsinki75.html

United Nations. (1978). *Final document of the tenth special session of the general assembly (first special session on disarmament 1978).* Retrieved from http://chnm.gmu.edu /1989/archive/files/helsinki-accords_f9de6be034.pdf

United Nations (1982). *Comprehensive study on confidence-building measures.* Retrieved from www.un.org/disarmament/HomePage/ODAPublications/DisarmamentStudy.

United Nations. (1984). *Document of the Stockholm conference.* Retrieved from http://www.osce.org/fsc/41238?download=false

United Nations. (1992). *Of the negotiations on confidence- and security-building measures convened in accordance with the relevant provisions of the concluding document of the Vienna meeting of the conference and security and co-operation in Europe.* Retrieved from http://www.fas.org/nuke/control/osce/text/VIENN92E.htm

United Nations Center for Disarmament. (1982). *The U.N. and disarmament: The second special session.* Retrieved from http://www.heritage.org/research/reports/1982/05/the-un-and-disarmament-the-second-special-session

U.S. Army. (2006). *Counterinsurgency, FM 3-24.* Retrieved from http://www.fas.org/irp /doddir/army/fm3-24.pdf

Van Dorn, R., Williams, J., Del-Colle, M., & Hawkins, J. (2009). Substance use, mental illness and violence: The co-occurrence of problem behaviors among young adults. *The Journal of Behavioral Health Services & Research, 36*(4), 465-77.

Vick, A. (1988). *Confidence-building during peace and war.* Retrieved from http://www.rand.org/pubs/notes/2009/N2698.pdf

Wagstaff, G., MacVeigh, J., Boston, R., & Scott, L., et al. (2003). Can laboratory findings on eyewitness testimony be generalized to the real world? An archival analysis of the influence of violence, weapon presence, and age on eyewitness accuracy. *The Journal of Psychology, 137*(1), 17-28.

Wareham, J., Boots, D., & Chavez, J. (2009). Social learning theory and intimate violence among men participating in a family violence intervention program. *Journal of Crime & Justice, 32*(1), 93.

Webb, K. (1992). Science, biology, and conflict. *Global Society,6*(1). Retrieved from http://www.tandfonline.com/doi/abs/10.1080/13600829208443014

Wolff, S. (2013). Confidence-building measures: An overview of elite-level options. Retrieved from http://www.stefanwolff.com/files/Confidence-building%20Measures.pdf

Woolford, A. & Ratner, R. (2009). Mediation frames/justice games. In D. Sandole, S. Byrne, I. Sandole-Staroste, & J. Senehi (Eds.) *Handbook of conflict analysis and resolution* (pp. 170-183). New York: Routledge.

Wright, J., Basco, M. & Thase, M.. (2006). *Learning cognitive-behavior therapy.* Washington, DC: American.

Yuan, J. (2011) Beijing's balancing act: Courting New Delhi, reassuring Islamabad. *Journal of International Affairs, 64*(2), 37-47.

Žagar, M. (2009). Strategies for the prevention, management, and/or resolution of (ethnic) crisis and conflict: The case of the Balkans. In D. Sandole, S. Byrne, I. Sandole-Staroste, & J. Senehi (Eds.) *Handbook of conflict analysis and resolution* (pp. 170-183). New York: Routledge.

Zepeda, S. (2006). Cognitive dissonance, supervision, and administrative team conflict. *The International Journal of Educational Management, 20*(3), 224-232.

Zumeta, Z. (2000). Styles of mediation: facilitative, evaluative, and transformative mediation. *Mediate.com.* Retrieved from http://www.mediate.com/articles/zumeta.cfm

Appendix A

Signed Permission Letter

US Army Combat Studies Institute
Truesdell Hall, 290 Stimson, Unit 1
Fort Leavenworth, Kansas 66027-1293

March 4, 2013

Aaron Bazin
41 Woodfin Road
Newport News, Virginia 23601

Subject: Permission to Utilize the Operational Leadership Experiences Database

Dear Mr. Bazin,

We are gratified that you have an interest in our OLE project and hope you find the interviews useful. All of these are in the public domain and do not require permission for use. Additionally, we have no prohibitions against you contacting the interviewees independently for follow-on research.

Sincerely,

Kendall D. Gott
Senior Historian, US Army Combat Studies Institute

Appendix B

Informed Consent Form

PLEASE SIGN, SCAN, AND RETURN THIS FORM

Study Title: Winning Hearts and Minds: A Grounded Theory Model for the Use of Confidence-building Measures in the Joint Operational Environment

IRB #13-010-O
Expiration Date: March 4, 2014

Dear Participant:

You are invited to participate in a research study that will attempt to understand the experiences of service members tasked with building trust with indigenous civilians and military personnel in Iraq and Afghanistan. The following information is provided in order to help you make an informed decision about your choice of participation. If you have any questions please do not hesitate to ask at any time. You are eligible to participate in this study because you are offering opinions as an individual based on your personal experiences, not as an official representative of the U.S. military or U.S. government.

Purpose of the Study: The purpose of this study is to construct a model of confidence-building measures as applied by service members in Iraq and Afghanistan for potential use by future service members.

Procedures: You will be asked to participate in an interview that will take approximately one hour of your time. The interview will be audio recorded and will take place over the phone or in a setting of your choice. During the interview, you will be asked a series of questions. These questions are designed to allow you to share your experiences and insights.

Risks: There are no known risks associated with this research.

Benefits: There is no monetary compensation for participation, however, your lessons learned in combat will go toward assisting future soldiers facing similar circumstances in the future.

Confidentiality: In the report you will be addressed by a number only. All documents will be kept in my files to ensure the confidentiality of your identity. All records obtained in this study will be kept confidential. There will not be any information that will be published that includes any identifying information about you. Research records will be stored securely and I will be the only one with access to the records. Your individual privacy will be maintained, should the study be presented in any publications or journals. All recordings will be destroyed five years after conclusion of this study. You are offering this information confidentially and it represents your own personal opinion and is not, nor will it be represented as, an official opinion of the military. No classified information will be discussed or recorded at any time.

Voluntary Participation: Participation in this study is voluntary. You may decide at any time to terminate your participation.

Opportunity to Ask Questions: You may ask any questions concerning this research and have those questions answered before agreeing to participate or anytime during the study. You may also contact my dissertation chair, Dr. xxxx, at xxxx@faculty.rockies.edu. Additionally, the University of the Rockies Institutional Review Board point of contact for this study is Dr. xxxx at xxxx@rockies.edu@rockies.edu.

Consent: If you wish to participate in this study, you will be interviewed. You are voluntarily making a decision whether or not to participate in this research study. Your signature below certifies that you have decided to participate and have read and understand the information presented. You will be given a copy of this consent form for your own personal records.

Signatures: I have been given information about this research study and its risks and benefits and have had the opportunity to ask questions and to have my questions answered to my satisfaction. I freely give my consent to participate in this research project.

_____   _____
Signature of Participant   Date

I hereby give consent for Aaron Bazin to record my interview.

_____   _____
Initials of Participant   Date

_____   _____
Signature of Researcher   Date

Aaron A. Bazin

Doctoral Candidate at the University of the Rockies, Colorado Springs, CO
Program: Organizational Leadership

Appendix C

Subject Matter Expert Interview Framework

1. Obtain approval and signature on informed consent form.

2. Biographic Information (First Name):

       Age:

       Rank:

       Sex:

       Specialty:

       Dates / Locations of Deployments:

3. Interview questions (with follow-up questions as required):

       a. Describe in detail the circumstances where, as part of your duties, you were required to build trust with local civilians or forces?

       b. Do you feel like you were successful in building trust, and why?

       c. How long does it take to really build trust, and why?

       d. What are the most important measures you used to build trust?

       e. In your opinion, what is the process of building trust, or is there a process at all?

       f. What advice would you give to other soldiers who may face similar circumstances in the future, what should they do, what should they never do?

       g. Please look at this diagram [show model to interviewee]. How accurately does this diagram depict how you used different measures to build trust? How should it be adjusted?

       h. In discussing the topic of building confidence and trust with local civilians or forces while deployed, what have we missed? What else needs to be addressed?

Appendix D

Subject Matter Expert Contact Email

SUBJECT: Request For Your Participation in a Research Study

NAME,

I read the interview that you gave for the Operational Leadership Experiences Project at Fort Leavenworth and I found it very insightful. I am conducting follow-up research for my doctoral dissertation on how soldiers built confidence with host-nation stakeholders in Iraq and Afghanistan.

Based on a review of over 2,500 interviews, I have identified you as an expert on the subject and I would like to ask you to consider completing an additional interview to captures your experience and will be of use to soldiers who face similar situations in the future. Your participation is strictly voluntary and we can do the interview over the phone. It should take less than hour of your time.

If you are able to participate, please print, sign, scan, and return the attached informed consent form and I will contact you to set up an interview time.

Thank you for your consideration. Please let me know if you have any questions.

Very Respectfully,

Aaron A. Bazin

Graduate Student University of the Rockies

ABOUT THE AUTHOR

Aaron is a career U.S. Army officer with over 20 years of leadership experience at the highest levels of the Department of Defense, the North Atlantic Treaty Organization, U.S. Central Command, and within the institutional Army. He holds a Doctorate in Psychology from the University of the Rockies, and a Masters of Business Administration from Liberty University. As an Army Strategist (Functional Area 59), he has successfully led numerous strategic and operational planning teams charged with tackling a wide variety of complex and dynamic problems. Aaron has served overseas in Pakistan, Afghanistan, Qatar, Iraq, Kuwait, Bahrain, and the United Arab Emirates. He is the recipient of the Bronze Star and the Combat Action Badge, among other military awards. Aaron has authored numerous professional articles on strategy development, defense planning, and conflict intervention. Aaron, his wife Julie, and their two children, Ryan and Emily, live in the Hampton Roads area of Virginia.

Linked In Profile: https://www.linkedin.com/in/aaron-bazin-b2923113

www.ingramcontent.com/pod-product-compliance
Lightning Source LLC
Chambersburg PA
CBHW081831280526
45789CB00007B/2414